D1572024

The
Steady
Way to
Greatness

Alicia Craybas

About the Author

Melanie Barnum is a psychic medium, intuitive counselor, life coach, hypnotist, and workshop presenter who has been practicing professionally for more than fifteen years. She is the author of *The Book of Psychic Symbols* and was a VIP reader at Psych-Out, a gathering of the nation's foremost psychics organized by Court TV. Barnum is also an Angelspeake Facilitator and a member of the National Guild of Hypnotists (NGH), as well as the International Association of Counselors and Therapists (IACT). She lives in Connecticut.

Visit her online at MelanieBarnum.com.

The
Steady
Way to
Greatness

· ·

Liberate Your Intuitive Potential
& Manifest Your Heartfelt Desires

MELANIE BARNUM

· ·

Llewellyn Publications
Woodbury, Minnesota

FIRST EDITION
First Printing, 2014

Cover background: iStock.com/23562559/iadamson
Cover design by Ellen Lawson
Interior illustrations by the Llewellyn Art Department

Llewellyn is a registered trademark of Llewellyn Worldwide Ltd.

Library of Congress Cataloging-in-Publication Data

Barnum, Melanie, 1969–
  The steady way to greatness : liberate your intuitive potential & manifest your heartfelt desires / Melanie Barnum. — First Edition.
      pages   cm
  Includes bibliographical references.
  ISBN 978-0-7387-3835-2
1. Success—Psychic aspects. 2. Intuition—Miscellanea. I. Title.
  BF1045.S83B37 2014
  158.1—dc23
                        2013035471

Llewellyn Worldwide Ltd. does not participate in, endorse, or have any authority or responsibility concerning private business transactions between our authors and the public.
  All mail addressed to the author is forwarded, but the publisher cannot, unless specifically instructed by the author, give out an address or phone number.
  Any Internet references contained in this work are current at publication time, but the publisher cannot guarantee that a specific location will continue to be maintained. Please refer to the publisher's website for links to authors' websites and other sources.

Llewellyn Publications
A Division of Llewellyn Worldwide Ltd.
2143 Wooddale Drive
Woodbury, MN 55125-2989
www.llewellyn.com

Printed in the United States of America

Also by Melanie Barnum

The Book of Psychic Symbols:
Interpreting Intuitive Messages

Dedication

My husband, Tom, and my daughters, Molly and Samantha, are what keep me going. They are my inspiration and my light. Without their love, encouragement, and belief in me, this book never would have been written. I am, indeed, awed by their greatness.

Acknowledgments

My mother, my best friend, always said, "Everyone has at least one good book in them." This I took to heart. Why not? I know she was there, smiling down, as I wrote this book and my first one, and is still there, sending love to my family and helping me with every reading I do. For that, and everything else you did for me, thank you, Mom! I love and miss you!

Being a psychic while maintaining normalcy every day can be quite the balancing act. For this, and so much more, I need to thank my husband, Tom, and my daughters, Molly and Samantha. My family is incredible. My girls are proud of their mama and think what I do is pretty cool. Samantha brags about her "psychic family," and Molly and her friends occasionally enlist my abilities to teach them and guide them as they navigate through their teenage years. My husband has stopped listening to my doubts, insisting I am much better in every way than I give myself credit for, and tells me he is extremely proud of me, especially because the work I do is not always welcomed or respected. His chest-puffing when talking about his wife is real. My family's genuine confidence in me and my gifts keeps me strong and, more importantly, happy.

A sincere "Thank you!" as well to Tammy Nelson, an incredible author, therapist, and speaker, and most importantly, my sister. Her greatness shines every day. Without her love and support, the difficult days may have been too hard to push through.

And to all of my friends, who are indeed part of my family: thank you for believing in me even when I have a hard time believing in myself! You've generated so much excitement to keep me going in my endeavors, and validated my gifts when I doubted them! You've challenged and encouraged and always been there to support me.

To all of the clients, friends, and family members who have shared a little piece of their lives with me, and now with all of you, thank you! Your stories will help so many to understand how every bit of real life affects us in so many ways. And, thanks to Alicia Craybas for using her time and energy to make me beautiful during our photo shoot.

My gratitude also goes out to every teacher who allowed me to share the energy of their classroom; this of course includes anyone who has ever taught me anything that has led me to this point in my life. Sincere thanks to every author and every psychic who has ever had the courage to put pen to paper to pave the way and spread knowledge and wisdom to so many, especially on topics that are not always respected.

My intuition showed me a moon on the binding of my first book before it was even written. I immediately doubted what I saw, knowing full well that Llewellyn was a very well-respected publishing house and a frontrunner in my genre. I thought there was no way they would publish my book. Thankfully, I ignored my doubt and instead sent them my first manuscript. They have more than validated their greatness with all of their hard work and dedication to me and all of the authors at Llewellyn. One person in particular deserves my gratitude! A great big thank you to Angela Wix! She has helped me, encouraged me, and answered my seemingly never-ending questions with a literary smile. And, thanks so much to Brett Fechheimer and all of the other staff at Llewellyn who have worked tirelessly to get this book, as well as my first, into the hands of what I hope will be millions! Enjoy!

Disclaimers

Throughout this book I have used stories and composites of stories designed to help the reader better understand the process. At times, some of the names, dates, or locations have been changed as well to ensure confidentiality and protect identities.

Throughout the book I talk about God and the universe. Understand that although I use these terms interchangeably, I fully intend for you, if you desire, to replace them with what you believe in or have faith in. My use of this terminology is in no way intended to discredit or deny your faith or beliefs, but is meant to allow all to feel and be included and to participate in every way.

Contents

List of Exercises

Introduction

Getting to Know Me and This Book

"I understand what you're saying, but I see major changes coming. I feel you manifesting greatness over the next couple of years. You are going to be making incredible changes that will help explain everything," I told my client Jim during a psychic reading session a few years back.

"What do you mean, 'manifest greatness'? I'm okay; I'm not great. I'm just a person. How can I possibly live up to that? How would that change my life?"

"I feel like your energy is building up. You are on the verge of something that is huge for you. That's what greatness is—your purpose, following your bliss. That's what it's all about," I continued.

"Well, I don't get it, and I don't understand. But whatever. So, do you see my job at the home-improvement store getting any better?" He changed the subject.

Jim *didn't* get it, he *didn't* understand—yet. And that was okay because I got it, and I saw his life changing for the better. I knew within the next two years he was going to be doing something drastically different, something that would transform his existence from

1

merely surviving to experiencing greatness. He was going to be healing people.

Soon after I'd given him his reading, he decided to take a course that changed his life. He began massage therapy and found that not only was he incredibly gifted, he also felt wonderful. He went on to include energy healing and meditation work. Jim had found his greatness; this is what made him feel tremendous joy, and what he was able to share with the world.

Let this be your year! We have all, at one time or another, wanted to change something in our lives. We've dreamt of greater successes or what those successes could do for us. We've all wished for an easy way for this to happen, but we rarely look within ourselves as a means to make this dream our reality. You have within you a greatness that is dying to break free! This greatness is there, bubbling to the surface, willing you to come forth and direct its path. Greatness is a state of being, something we all possess but few ever achieve. It is a blossoming of our natural potential, which allows us to feel liberated and exhilarated, connecting us to the universe.

It is simple, really, the idea of making life better. It is something we strive for, an accomplishment to achieve no matter our age, race, gender, or nationality. It is part of a natural desire to improve and, yes, have an abundant and fulfilling existence. There is absolutely no shame in wanting to be or be part of something great. We all have it; we just don't always realize it.

Who I am

I am psychic. I am also an intuitive counselor, medium, hypnotist, and energy healer. I regularly work with clients from all walks of life over the phone and out of my Ridgefield, Connecticut, office to help them understand their lives, their purpose in life, and to make any changes they deem necessary so they may live a more rewarding life. I do individual readings and group sessions, and I enjoy helping people and connecting them to themselves and their deceased loved ones. I am there to facilitate their greatness as well.

Almost two decades ago I felt like I was actually hit over the head and I heard the words, "You need to do this work now!" I couldn't possibly imagine why I was being singled out or how the heck I would ever be able to "do this work now," but I knew it had happened for a reason. So, I set out to learn everything I could and took dozens of workshops and classes and began my journey, absorbing all the information about psychic gifts, intuition, and manifesting that I could along the way. Though a very rational person, I was open to the possibility there was more to life than what I was currently experiencing. Having been an accountant, and at the time a store owner, I was more grounded in logic and reason than intuition and whatever else was floating around in the ether. But I recognized I had an ability to understand people's energy my whole life, even though I'd never classified it as intuition, since I thought everyone did the same thing. After all, I was normal.

Why this book? What's in it for me?

Normalcy has changed for me since being hit over the head with what I now consider my wake-up call, or should I say wake-up bat. Over the past sixteen or so years of working professionally, I've come to realize something invaluable; something that has been staring me in the face forever. Through intuition, we have the power to manifest what we want, and furthermore we can, every one of us, achieve a level of greatness that surpasses our wildest imaginings. But there is a catch. In order to manifest anything external, or more importantly internal, we need to tune in to our intuition so we can understand any impressions we have or we receive from the universe of what our life could be and how incredible it can become. Our intuition allows us to recognize these impressions for what they are: clues to help us manifest.

There is a difference between the actual "act of manifesting" and "how to manifest." Within the pages of this book are directions and exercises focused on the act of manifesting: what it is, how to do it, and why you'd want to. The act of manifesting is extremely important to our ability to achieve goals and become successful. To manifest usually means to create or bring something into your life that is not presently there. This is different from "the how." Sometimes, to manifest simply means to unveil or recognize something that is currently within us to a degree that we become aware of its existence. The something I consider crucial and am talking about here is "greatness." It is already inside you, this greatness, and is just waiting to bloom.

Throughout my almost two decades of doing psychic readings, energy work, and teaching, I have been tapping into my own greatness—what I was born to do to bring abundance and joy of every kind into my own life and the lives of those around me. Living in this greatness is my purpose; it's what feels comfortable, exciting, rewarding, immensely satisfying, and just plain right. This is my greatness. It is different from success and different from my career. This and being a mother to my beautiful children is what makes me tick, what makes me feel at one with the universe. I am sure this is my greatness.

Your greatness is there, waiting for you to become aware of it. The potential resides within you. You've already taken the first step to discovering it by reading this book. Within these pages you'll learn about both the act of manifesting things and how, also, to manifest or bring out your own greatness.

"Why," you may ask, "would I want to?"

The answer is simple. Now that you know of the potential within you to feel and be incredible, you will be unable to forget about it. We are all inherently intuitive beings. We utilize this intuition in a variety of ways, though we don't always recognize it. Our intuition helps guide us and direct us through this crazy world, and when we listen to our gut instincts, we traverse happily. Using our intuition, letting it help steer us toward our higher purpose, bridges the distance between knowing about greatness and achieving or manifesting our own greatness. Without our intuition to channel or even funnel us in the right direction, we may be stuck floundering, never reaching our potential and never knowing what we truly can manifest. It is this combination of manifesting and intuition that not only helps us discover our greatness but also keeps us from succumbing to a tedious life filled with boredom and monotony.

Often we want to realize our goals and desires immediately. And at times that works. More often than not, though, it takes time and patience. By using the steps in this book, you will find the path is actually part of the achievement. You will be able to enjoy the ride and won't only need to look forward to the destination, as you'll manifest your desires during the trip.

Throughout the next fifty-two weeks, you will create a change that will be everlasting. You may choose to do the fifty-two exercises in a row, rather than letting them play out over the year. And that's fine. Certainly there are some that will lend themselves to quickening the process. Just be sure to give yourself enough time to truly appreciate the experiences you will have while doing the exercises! Regardless of which way you decide to use the book, along the way you will determine what manifesting greatness truly means to you.

Just as there are many facets to a diamond in the rough, there are many parts to your life, and by extension, many challenges to address in order to create a life you are excited to wake up to every morning. The variety of sections in this book will aid you in detailing the necessary, intriguing, and even fun steps that will get you to that place.

By tuning in to your intuition, you will understand where your energy goes, and what it means to direct your intentions. You'll also become aware of the part your intuition plays in understanding the symbolic messages you will receive to help you manifest what you truly desire. Your energetic footprint will be easier to recognize after you separate the positive from the negative, and you'll identify how these forces feel in your body, mind, and spirit.

We are not all born knowing exactly what we want to accomplish. Most of us need some help! It's not as though you chose your purpose in life as you took your first breath. You will come to learn what motivates you to achieve your desires and, alternatively, what holds you back from reaching those goals. By visualizing exactly what you want, the intensity of your desires will increase, allowing the universe to be directed toward precisely what it is you wish for. If your intentions are for your greatest good, your wishes will be fulfilled.

You cannot create a better life until you modify how you are living now. Identifying your strengths will help you understand what motivates you to want to change. Transformation is easier when we use our strengths instead of our weaknesses. We pour in positive energy that way, keeping the negative energy from overpowering us.

Each week you will tap into your potential by using unique exercises created specifically to take you on a journey to understanding your greatness. Though designed to enhance your experience over the course of a year, if you have the desire to speed up the process, it is truly within your grasp. Work at your own pace, secure in the knowledge that you can go back to and repeat the exercises as often as you'd like.

You are about to enter into the process of manifesting greatness. Complementary to that, you have the opportunity to manifest other desires along the way to achieving greatness that will help you more fully enjoy your destiny. In addition to each week's exercise, you will have weekly steps called *Manifesting* exercises. With these, you will not only be practicing your manifesting techniques, but you will also be creating and bringing into your life a variety of wishes, including everyday desires as well as long-term abundance.

For each weekly *Manifesting* exercise, there are icons included to instruct you either to write down ✑ what it's telling you to do, say the phrase out loud ☺, or perform a manifestation action ☆. For each one that you're guided to write down, use a separate piece of paper and write it over and over, until you feel you're done.

You should get a special box where you can keep all of your manifesting papers for the year. When it's a "say it out loud," you can think of it as an affirmation to repeat at least ten times immediately and then continue to repeat it throughout the week. For each "action" icon, well that's easy—just do it. At the end of the year, empty your box and read them all out loud. Go back over all of your *Manifesting* exercises and make note of which have come to fruition, which you no longer want, and which you feel you've not yet achieved.

Overall, think of this book as a means to discover who you are, what you want, and who you can become. You may use it as a guide to assist you in tapping into your true potential and as a digest directed toward self-improvement. Right now, in your current state, you are merely existing, hopefully enjoying life, but with an innate potential for so much more. The insight you will gain from this book will help you blossom, flourish, and accomplish your goals. Utilizing the many exercises within these pages will help you open to your intuition and your incredible ability to manifest.

After you've followed all fifty-two of the steps, you will be ready to begin to live the rest of your life from a new place of absolute contentedness. Everything will align itself in the right pattern and design for the universe to help fulfill your requests, and you will begin to manifest greatness! One of the hardest parts is taking the plunge; after all, that means change. Change can be scary sometimes. But don't ever forget … change can be awesome. Les Brown, a motivational speaker who went from having next to nothing to being extremely successful, shared an important idea: "You don't have to be great to get started, but you've got to get started to be great!"

• •

WEEK 1 EXERCISE:
GET STARTED!

Over the next seven days, find new and different places to get comfortable while reading this book. Take note of where and what time of day you feel the most relaxed and most able to really tune in to the book as you read it. Do you feel best reading while lying down in bed at night? Are you more content sitting on the couch while you read? At the dining room table? What about the local coffeehouse? Outside on a blanket at the park? Or even on your lunch break with your office door closed? Make an effort to continue reading where you feel the most at ease, as this will help you do the exercises in the book. If you can't be in that particular spot all the time, no worries; take that same feeling of comfort with you to the other locations.

As you read, go back over the parts that you feel you need to in order to reach a deeper understanding or that you may have a question or two about. Allow yourself the leisure of reading for pure enjoyment. Make your way through the book with or without participating in any of the exercises the first time around.

Get yourself a journal. You will have plenty of opportunities to record your thoughts, desires, answers, and more with all of the exercises to come! Make sure you have plenty of pages in your journal; over 100 will probably be necessary. Or, you may choose the alternative method of typing directly into a word-processing document. Either way is fine, though you will at some point need an actual pen and paper; be sure those are handy.

Above all, enjoy it! This book is not meant to be difficult, though you may find yourself having a hard time letting go or giving in to some of the exercises.

Remember, this is the first step in *Manifesting Greatness*!

Manifesting

"This book is my tool for manifesting my personal greatness!"

✍ ☺

. . . .

What Is "Manifesting Greatness"?

We all have within us the capacity to manifest greatness. Simply stated, this means we possess the potential to create something in our lives that will bring us extreme pleasure or good fortune. This is something that feels right in our hearts and our souls. It's something budding, waiting to bloom; it's already within us. We need only determine what that greatness is.

Manifesting greatness does not simply mean we create one thing, one act, or one random blip in the universe. It means we have the ability to change our lives through this manifestation. The key to creating the change is to decide exactly what our potential for greatness is.

For some, greatness can represent stardom—a chance to live in the limelight and be worshipped by many. For others, achieving greatness may suggest becoming a parent for the first time, possibly after many failed attempts. And still others can become incredible humanitarians, helping without expecting anything in return. Regardless of what greatness represents, it means the same thing: an impressive, exceptional, influential state.

Manifesting greatness is not just about striking it rich, though that can be part of it. It is more a blossoming of our soul. We have within us potential. This potential varies from person to person, or soul to soul. Just as we are all one-of-a-kind people, we all possess unique traits to help us reach something of bigger significance, something attainable by each individual exclusively.

This greatness does not simply occur without any thought or contemplation. It is a state of being, of knowing who we are and what we want our lives to be. Manifestation is the creation of something or attracting what it is that we wish for. This means that manifesting greatness is the act of designing and creating an incredible state of being that far surpasses merely existing and brings with it an indescribable joy. This is what manifesting greatness can be.

We are meant to be great

There is a thing deep down inside each of us, a niggling perhaps, the tiniest flutter of an idea or a thought that we want to be something great or do something huge with our life. This is not a new concept. This is something we are born with, that we nurture as children and have encouraged by adults and teachers. Unfortunately, we forget. We let reality creep in, and this dream, this belief, takes a back seat to the pressures of growing up and fitting in. We underestimate this butterfly-like feeling we have that tells us we were born to accomplish more.

I had a new client in last week, Kelly. She had a great psychic reading session and left the office. The next day, I received an email. She loved the reading but wanted more. Kelly was looking to be mentored. She felt, intuitively, there was something she was so close to, but she couldn't quite figure out what it was. Kelly knew her life was getting ready to change, and was eager but frustrated because she was unable to decipher what she needed to do to change it. She was ready. So, we began exploring her potential for greatness.

This feeling is not uniquely hers. This is something many of us experience. It is a searching; a longing inside for what we feel will ultimately fulfill us. Once we've decided to put our energy into achieving our goals, we can begin to understand them. Abraham Lincoln pointed out, "If we magnified our successes as much as we magnify our disappointments, we'd all be much happier." Confusion surfaces because we don't know what our particular greatness is. But there need not be confusion while we continue our search to fulfill it. We must explore the potential within us and amplify it out to the world.

Dare to dream

At a class I was recently teaching, Marisa shared something.

"I don't believe in dreams anymore. My dreams all of a sudden stopped. After I got married and had kids, I no longer had any dreams of my future. I am not sure why. Also, my intuition doesn't seem to be there anymore either."

After she said this, I was surprised, though I shouldn't have been, by the number of *uh-huh*s and *me too*s I was hearing. As I looked around the room, it was pretty obvious to me that the other fifty or so students had stopped believing in dreams as well.

They chimed in, "Why is this? Why does this happen? What does it mean?" The answer was quite simple, really. They had stopped believing in the possibilities. They no longer put together that you have to believe it to achieve it and that their fear of success may be preventing them from even formulating the simplest goals.

We then went on to explore how their intuition could help them rekindle their desires and dreams. By looking at their circumstances from a new perspective, they began tuning in to their intuition to figure out what it was they had forgotten, and what their dreams could now be. The class came to the conclusion that they had been brought together by a series of fortunate circumstances, also known as synchronicity, and that they were in the right place at the right time to change their lives.

When we were young, we were asked what we wanted to be when we grew up. We responded with statements like, "I want to be a firefighter," "I want to be a doctor," "I want to be a police officer," "I want to travel the world and help people who can't help themselves," "I want to write an amazing book," "I want to dance," "I want to be a star." You don't generally hear, "I want to work the night shift at the mini-mart" or "I want to pump out septic systems." Not that these professions are bad; the world needs everyone, and I'm thankful to have a place to shop and have my tank pumped. But they are not necessarily the things most people aspire to be. Circumstances or convenience places us in these positions; these, generally, are not our grand dreams or desires as children.

Those dreams of children commonly get squashed. We are directed to be practical more often than we are encouraged to be different. We need to pick a college major or a job that will have benefits. We need something now that will provide for our families, put food on the table, and give us a steady paycheck just so we can live—hand to mouth. We are told we can be anything we want to be, but always with the caveat that it has to be within reason.

Why? Why do we compromise? When we are children, we do as we're told, but as adults we can pursue what we want. Do we stop actively chasing that dream for fear we will lose it? Or, do we cut short our imaginings because we are afraid we will forfeit everything else? Are we so scared of failure that we won't even try for success? Have we created a life for ourselves and our loved ones that leaves us no other option? Are we in such a hurry that we can't allow ourselves the time to pursue what we truly desire? I think, possibly, the answer is all of the above.

More than great

I had a conversation with a friend, Darrell. He stated he never liked the words *great* or *greatness*. For him, they held negative connotations. They represented the end, the finish line. "Once you've achieved greatness, there's nothing more," he stated. He believed the mere words suggested we had nothing left to accomplish and therefore we would be done; life would have reached its end game, taken its final stand. The breath within us would be exhaled and we would expire...for good.

My response was simple. I believe greatness is all around us, traveling as energy through us, connecting us all and making us a never-ending part of the universe. I told him we owe it to the universe and to ourselves to blossom with that potential, to bring forth the best we are able to. I explained further that we will fit better within our bodies, our skin, when we strive to maximize our potential. When we are not fighting with our destinies, we are flowing more freely, without as many obstacles, hardships, or roadblocks to climb; less effort is needed to achieve more than ever before.

We agreed and we understood each other's ideas. I was able to comprehend Darrell's belief of greatness being the inevitable end, that there was nothing more after achieving it. And, luckily for both of us, Darrell was able to think through my explanation that we are all incredible souls, living and breathing as one in this existence. He was able to grasp the concept that we have the capacity to bring forth a miraculous greatness within ourselves that connects us and helps us be part of the universe instead of merely renting time and space. In the end, I think we both felt the same way; we just had different interpretations of what greatness really was. For me, it is the realization of something awesome; for him, it was the completion of that same something awesome.

Now is the chance you've been waiting for, the opportunity we've all dreamt of in one way or another. Now is the time to take action, to change the rest of your life in a way that will open up possibilities you've never imagined, let alone believed feasible. In the unlikely event you are still not convinced, try to imagine how it could benefit you to put in just a little bit of effort, without having to change everything in your life.

If you, like most people, are working only to bring home a paycheck, merely existing without truly living, it's time for you to make a commitment to yourself. You deserve to do more than just survive. You are entitled to immense happiness, and to share that overwhelming emotion with all of those you touch throughout your life. You are worthy of magnificence. You need only believe it to achieve it. Now's your chance to manifest greatness!

. . . .

WEEK 2 EXERCISE:

THINK BACK!

Get out your journal and turn to the first page. Write, "My dreams, my beliefs, and my obstacles" on the top of the page. Be sure to date this and every entry to come.

What were your childhood dreams? What did you believe possible as a child? What did you want to be when you grew up? Give yourself at least a paragraph in your journal for each question to write down your answers and to remember. After you're done writing, review your answers. Is there anything you need to add? Anything you forgot or want to change?

Now comes the hard part. What were your obstacles? Were there outside influences that changed your mind? Were you not appreciated or were your dreams not allowed by adults or others around you? Were you brought up believing you weren't worthy? Again, be sure to record your answers and allow a minimum of at least one paragraph per question.

Throughout the week, revisit the questions and see if there is anything else you wish to add. Make a note of any feelings or memories you have regarding any of the questions.

Manifesting

It's time to get your groove on! Get out there one day this week and, for a short time, live as if you've realized your childhood dreams! Use your imagination and act as if you were the person you thought you would be when you grew up. If you thought you would be a famous actress, dress up and go out for a night on the town! If you wanted to be a firefighter, go to the local firehouse and ask if you can do a ride-along. If you wanted to be a photographer, go take pictures—lots of them! It's not too late to live your dreams!

. . . .

. . . .

Chapter 1

Greatness

(WEEKS 3–6)

What You Believe about Success

Most of us have a preconceived notion or an idea of what success is. Usually, this involves money. More specifically, it involves having a lot of money. Success, we've learned, is about working diligently at a job that we may or may not like in order to make as much cash as we possibly can. The *Encarta* dictionary defines *success* as "the achievement of intention; [the] attainment of fame, wealth, or power; something that turns out well; somebody successful: somebody who is wealthy, famous, or powerful because of a record of achievement." This is a description most of us would agree on.

Success can also be described as reaching the top rung on the social-status ladder. Achieving fame within your socially accepted group can raise you to a new level. This attainment can create a feeling of being above it all, and it can suggest a belief that you are better than the rest, and therefore more successful.

Successful living

There are, however, many people, including me, who would beg to differ when asked for their interpretation. I think success is about being happy and creating a life you enjoy living. I emphatically believe success is also about sharing that happiness with family—more specifically, having the ability or wherewithal to extend joy throughout the lives of your partner, your children, and your friends. Theodore Roosevelt explained how kids are one's greatest successes when he said, "For unflagging interest and enjoyment, a household of children, if things go reasonably well, certainly makes all other forms of success and achievement lose their importance by comparison."

What you think about success is important. It goes beyond a simple childhood wish to be famous or wealthy; it categorizes how you judge failures and victories in adulthood. What we accept as truth becomes translated in how we relate to others we interact with. Challenging others to reach our standards becomes the norm, and if they don't attain that level of achievement, we judge them as unworthy or even sometimes unnecessary.

Take, for example, the homeless man who is panhandling on the street. Do you, like many, judge him or think he is unfit or less of a man because he is begging for change? Do you find yourself feeling a bit uncomfortable the closer he gets to your own personal space? In a society that looks to monetary wealth as a gauge for successful living, it is normal to experience those emotions. It doesn't make them wrong or right.

However, perhaps that man is begging for change because he had an extraordinarily unfavorable turn of events. Maybe he was wealthy, but lost it all when the market crashed. Does that diminish his capacity for success? Does it mean he is now a lesser person? Would you deny his previous financial successes because of his current situation?

Success kudos

We are a fickle bunch. The example on the previous page was a great depiction of how we judge each other by what we hold to be true about wealth and power. We place value on financial gains rather than the achievement of our intentions, and we deem this successful.

This is not always the case. Losing weight is always admired, unless of course you are too thin already. Winning a marathon is a huge accomplishment. Becoming a published author is a major triumph. Getting a raise is worth a celebration. We accept that there will always be successes within our lives. But do these achievements make us successful?

With our kids we actually pay attention to the little things in life. We allow that our children are successful when they learn to use the potty for the first time. We praise their successes when they receive an A on their report card. We also congratulate them on scoring the goal that won the game. These are successes because they are incredible milestones in our kids' lives. They are not yet expected to be financially secure or financially independent. We don't need them to overcompensate for their lack of a bank account. We can celebrate their victories because we don't expect their triumphs to be monetarily related—yet. All of that will come later.

Success should feel pleasurable. It should not feel painful. Even if you are richer than you could have imagined in your wildest dreams, if you live in a state of emotional grief or unhappiness, that is not success. Anthony Robbins, life coach and self-help author, spoke of the importance of being happy: "I cannot emphasize strongly enough that what you link pain and pleasure to will shape your destiny." On a very fundamental level, we experience pleasure when we are successful in something we enjoy. If we are merely prosperous without enjoyment, is it really success? Being prosperous doesn't mean we should stop striving for fulfillment.

Years ago, I had a client who came in on a regular basis for intuitive and hypnotism coaching. Vince had a successful career as a high-earning executive. His sessions were spent exploring how he could become more successful in his job to increase his happiness. After many intuitive nudges from me, he finally realized what he really wanted was to start his own business and move to Vermont. He had never considered any other opportunities or desires because he felt the only way to achieve success was to be a wealthy businessman. The last time I heard from him, he was incredibly happy, enjoying the outdoors and running his Internet business from his new home. He is still financially independent, but now he appreciates his life. He is content.

The spiritual leader of Tibet and peacemaker around the world, His Holiness the Dalai Lama, exclaimed, "The planet does not need more successful people. The planet desperately needs more peacemakers, healers, restorers, storytellers, and lovers of all kinds." I understand that to mean the peacemakers, healers, restorers, storytellers, and lovers of all kinds *are* the successful people. Manifesting greatness in your life does not need to be defined by financial achievements. Limiting your greatness to this will never allow you to achieve the potential of who you can be.

Determining how you evaluate success is important. It can change the way you approach greatness. It can help or hinder you on the road to your personal manifestation of greatness. Knowing you have a birthright to be successful in your own life is an incredible feeling. Understanding your idea of success is the first step in manifesting greatness in your life.

· ·

WEEK 3 EXERCISE:

SUCCESS!

Open your journal to a new section and write down the word *Success*. Next, list every single word you can think of that describes it. Be sure you record every word you can imagine, even if it's only meaningful to you personally, that makes you think of success.

After you've done that, go down the list one by one. Read the first word aloud and then close your eyes. Taste the word. Pay attention to how it feels in your body when you say it again. Does it resonate with you? Do you still find it meaningful? If so, put a checkmark next to it. If not, put a single line through it. Continue with each word until you are all the way through the list.

Then, go back and do it again. Look at each word that has a checkmark next to it and do it again. Continue in this manner until you are sure you are satisfied with the words that are still there.

Finally, rewrite those words into one complete list.

Open your journal every day for a week and read the words aloud. If something doesn't feel right, or if you've changed your mind about the remaining words, cross them off. Otherwise, put another checkmark next to them.

Which words have checkmarks? Does this make sense to you? Does your idea of success feel different than it did before?

Manifesting

"I am successful because I am _____."

✍ ☺

• •

Rethinking What You Believe about Success

Our beliefs about success and greatness don't have to be written in stone. They can, instead, be written in sand. We can allow our ideas, opinions, and thoughts to change as we mature and grow in mind, body, and spirit. Our definition can morph and be transformed as we discover who we want to be and why. We need only to rethink what we previously thought. Then, maybe our opinion of what it means to be successful can be adjusted.

Rationalizing who we've become plays a big part in the modification of our limiting opinions. We start off with dreams of creating a perfect world and settle for running a company. This becomes our new idea of success. We are happy to have attained this new level of power, though it's not necessarily what we set out to achieve. But we don't always have to downgrade what success means. Sometimes our ideas about success shift.

Don't do anything strictly to be successful; just do what you love and believe in, and success will come naturally. The role we play in life can guide us down a path we enjoy or a path we'd rather not travel. When we love our job, it is no longer work. This is success in its purest form: the notion that we like what we do so much that we actually look forward to it. Our careers occupy a huge portion of our lives. When we can do them with enjoyment, it's a blessing.

We may also view success differently than our neighbor does. When I do psychic readings, there is generally a common theme. People ask about money, their career, their families, and their health—usually in that order. Does this mean they value money and their career above their families and their health? Not necessarily, but it may suggest they think they need money and a strong career to take care of their family and their health.

When they ask about their job, the question is usually the same: "Will I be successful?" This is interesting because every client is different. Their opinion of success often differs from mine, and generally differs from person to person. Yet when I tune in to their energy, I'm able to pick up on what they believe their level of success is.

Welcome it

I had a client ask me, "I am traveling to California to give a speech. How do you think it's going to go? Do you think it will be successful?" Now, what she really meant was did I see her getting a lot of work from it and, by extension, a lot of money. What I saw for her was it would be highly successful; she would be well received and the crowd would really enjoy what she had to say. I didn't feel this would bring her an abundance of money, though. When I explained this to her, she decided to cancel the trip.

"Why are you going to withdraw from the conference? People will love you there," I shared with her.

"Well, what's the point if it's not going to bring money in right away?"

I would have gone. I would have loved it. Making others happy and sharing what I'm continually learning would have brought me one step further toward my version of success. For her, it would have just set her back a week and would have been a waste of time, even though she was already financially abundant and didn't need to make money off of the conference.

It is said that successful people can sometimes be harsh in thought and action. Is this because the almighty dollar becomes more powerful and more important than all else? Having financial freedom to do the things we love is a definite plus. But should this be the be-all and end-all?

What if there was no one else to appreciate your success? Would you still feel successful? We have a kind of social hierarchy. If there were no one above you or beneath you on this imaginary scale, would you even notice your success? Would this change how you felt about success or your views on what success meant?

Scrooged

Take, for example, Ebenezer Scrooge from Dickens' 1843 novel, *A Christmas Carol*. He was financially abundant yet extremely miserable. He had no one to share his wealth and power with. People feared him, but only because he was mean and cantankerous and controlled most of the money in the town. He mistakenly believed this was the way it was supposed to be. His employee Bob Cratchit knew better. Though he and his family were destitute, they had something more powerful than money: they had love. It wasn't until Ebenezer was shown a different way of life that he changed, and changed for the better. In the end, it was the sharing of his wealth and power that ultimately made him successful and happy.

Success does not always equal money, and sometimes it's hard to remember that. Being financially secure is not a bad thing, however. There is no reason we need to be poor to be successful. We can achieve financial *and* spiritual abundance. Prosperity can actually help us become better people. Money doesn't make everything all better, but it certainly helps. It can reduce the worrying over if there's enough money to pay the rent or the mortgage. It eases our stress regarding our children on a fundamental level: we can feed them, clothe them, shelter them, and keep them relatively safe. Financial security is not something to be scorned at; it is just not the only thing we should strive for.

Albert Einstein, an amazing man with a brilliant mind, said it best: "Try not to become a man of success but rather try to become a man of value." What we value varies greatly from person to person. The wonderful thing is our values can change as we evolve. We need only make the effort to rethink them.

- -

WEEK 4 EXERCISE:

RETHINK SUCCESS!

Take a deep breath; this is going to get tough! You are going to reframe your idea about success. Turn to a fresh page in your

journal and write "Rethinking Success." In your current state of affairs, there are certain goals you wish to accomplish. They can be simple goals, such as getting a paycheck at the end of the week or not getting fired, or bigger goals like getting a part in an upcoming television show. Be sure to write down every goal you can possibly think of.

Next, write down your goals as if you had absolutely no responsibilities and could be or do whatever you wanted. These could include great aspirations like becoming president of the United States or meditating with the Dalai Lama, or your dreams could portray you as a business tycoon like Donald Trump.

Now, after you've recorded every possible goal—both the simpler, more realistic ones and the greatest you could imagine—review them. Notice which revolve around financial success and which don't. Categorize them using descriptions such as "Financial," "Spiritual," "Familial," "Body, Mind, Spirit," and so on. Look over each category and examine whether these are new thoughts on success or the same ones you previously had. What's changed? What's stayed the same? Over the next week, revisit these themes and think about whether there is anything you'd like to remove or that no longer fits with what you view as successful. Also, add anything you may have previously excluded from your goals or your categories. We are very fluid people; our desires and wants can change many times over the course of even just one week.

Finally, on the last day of the week, take each item, goal by goal, and imagine how it would feel to attain it. Sit for at least five minutes per goal, and really allow yourself to experience how it affects your body, mind, and spirit to have achieved each desire.

Manifesting

"I will reach my goal of _____

by this date _____."

· ·

Identifying Great People

Successful people are flourishing for a reason. What is it they all share? They know what they want. They are not floundering through life; they are charging through, on a clear-cut course of their own making. Their version of success also has a common theme. Fame and power are still key ingredients to being recognized as successful, but we can't discount happiness. One is not truly successful unless one is happy.

You rock!

There are many famous successful people. We have genius minds like Bill Gates and television moguls like Oprah Winfrey. Presidents, royalty, actors, musicians, and professional athletes also share a claim to fame. These people had to work for what they wanted. They set out to do something spectacular, and they accomplished it. Sure, there's luck and lineage thrown in, but their greatness was not accomplished by sheer fortune alone. They created their lives; they didn't just let their lives happen.

There are also amazingly generous humanitarians and famous philanthropists—people who give of themselves through time, money, and reputation to assist others who need help. Many have crossed the categories of both fame and philanthropy, such as Paul Newman, Warren Buffett, and J. K. Rowling. Gandhi and Mother Teresa were great humanitarians, with no personal benefit other than comfort in knowing their benevolence helped others. This is greatness, this is success:

knowing you are meant to contribute to the well-being of others, and doing so with kindness and integrity.

Dolly Parton, the famous singer and humanitarian, shared her wisdom: "Find out who you are and do it on purpose." People who are able to determine what they really love have a huge advantage over everyone else. Pursuing that love or those interests enables them to create what they desire, instead of merely surviving with what they're given.

Never judge a book by its cover

Identifying those who have conquered their fears and become successful is not always easy. At first glance, we assume that people who present themselves well are successful; fancy cars, expensive jewelry and clothing, and a style to kill for are usually dead giveaways. But there is more to identifying a genuinely successful person.

Like the old adage says, "Never judge a book by its cover." We don't know what is inside the person's mind, in their thoughts. We can only wonder what is in their dreams. So, then, how can we possibly perceive that someone is great? It shows in their eyes, their smile, and their attitude.

Someone who is genuinely happy with who they are and where they are in life will exude greatness. They emanate a magnetic energy that makes others want to be near them. They will not need to stomp on someone else's dreams or beliefs in order to achieve their own. A successful person will be authentic, sharing whatever they have to help contribute to the personal wellness and contentment of others. And, above all, as Oscar Wilde suggested, "Be yourself; everyone else is already taken."

Successful people are innovative. They don't wait for others to create something and merely imitate them. They develop and follow through with plans of their own design, well-thought-out plans with specific goals. From conception, their ideas are groundbreaking; they are not afraid to take risks to achieve what they believe to be worthy.

You are amazing

Sometimes, it takes others to help us identify the greatness within. We assume we are average, because we are the ones living our own life. My mother used to tell me all the time that I didn't recognize how beautiful I was because the image looking back in the mirror was so "common" to me; I saw it every day. Just like this mirror story, we look to others to help us validate our greatness—not out of vanity, but because we truly don't see it. E. E. Cummings explained how we grow by believing in who we are: "We do not believe in ourselves until someone reveals that deep inside us something is valuable, worth listening to, worthy of our trust, sacred to our touch. Once we believe in ourselves, we can risk curiosity, wonder, spontaneous delight, or any experience that reveals the human spirit."

Recognizing our greatness is sometimes easier when we view it next to those we aspire, or merely desire, to be like. We emulate those we admire. Usually, admiration abounds when we are in the presence of greatness. Determining who we believe to be successful can assist us in understanding how we, ourselves, can be great.

• •

WEEK 5 EXERCISE:
WHO DO YOU THINK IS GREAT?

In your journal, write "Great People" in a fresh section. Then, begin listing people who come to mind. They can be people who are known for their athletic prowess or those known for their genius minds. You may also relate to some humanitarians or philanthropists. Record also any famous actors, singers, or performers if you feel they fit your parameters for greatness.

Now, and this is important, write down the names of people you think are great who are not famous! They can be parents, teachers, or mentors. They may be your local hero or someone who's fought illness and been a role model for others.

After you've listed the names, review them one by one and write down what you believe makes them great. Possibly this will include the public's view on why they are successful, but also be sure to record why *you* think each of these people is admirable or great.

Review what you've written. If there is anyone you've noted who doesn't seem to meet your criteria for greatness, cross off his or her name. They no longer need to be part of your list. Add any other traits you can think of for your great people until you've exhausted your thoughts.

Over the next week, visit this list daily. Begin noticing which qualities you've listed that resonate most with you and who you are. Circle those traits. Toward the end of the week, take that list of circled words and write them down in a new list. Do they represent qualities you would like to have? Or, are they traits that you believe contribute to greatness? If they don't, cross them off, delete them. Narrow down your inventory to include only the most prevalent descriptions, the traits you feel ring most true for you.

Focus on the remaining list and decide whether you already possess the qualities you respect. If so, super! You are on your way. If not, don't worry! By the end of these fifty-two weeks, you will!

Bonus!

Go back to your checkmarked list from earlier in this chapter. Do any of these match up with the traits you've circled during this exercise? Create a new list that contains the traits or words that are included from both chapters and explore how they feel to you.

Manifesting

"Starting this moment, the quality I am most happy to have is _____."

(Insert the quality you feel is essential
for you to possess in order to manifest greatness)

☺

. . . .

What Fulfillment Feels Like

When we have what we want, we experience a feeling. This sensation is like nothing else you've ever felt before. Think about being in school and getting the boy or the girl that you really liked. They asked you out, or they said yes when you asked them out. You felt exhilarated and happy; inside your tummy the butterflies were flapping. There was a sense of anticipation that equals no other.

We experience these intense emotions because we've won, we've succeeded, and we feel special. Getting a good grade after working hard to earn it gives us a sense of accomplishment. Scoring a goal after practicing for just that moment becomes more meaningful than making any random shot. Trying, without being deterred by possible failure, is what gives us that feeling. If we don't try, we can't ever experience success.

"Far better is it to dare mighty things, to win glorious triumphs even though checkered by failure, than to rank with those poor spirits who neither enjoy nor suffer much because they live in the gray twilight that knows neither victory nor defeat," Theodore Roosevelt said, and it still holds true. How can we possibly know success without first experiencing defeat?

Follow your bliss

What makes you happy? Following your bliss brings you on a path of self-discovery. Along the way you are able to challenge yourself. Self-motivation kicks in as you begin the makeover from the person you were to the person you long to become. This transformation ushers in self-awareness, and you realize you don't need to manufacture greatness. Rather, you need only commit to carrying out the changes, and it begins to feel right.

The key to happiness has been a question posed throughout time by just about every single person on the planet. There are, indeed, the little uplifting minutes of joy you get by doing something fun, like swinging on a swingset or singing at a concert with thousands of your closest friends while you rock out to the newest, most phenomenal band, or even eating the perfect ice cream cone on a beautiful summer day with the person or people you love the most. These are moments that everyone should experience regularly! But truly realizing your joy in life? That's a different type of feeling altogether. It can be breathtaking.

In his book *The Seven Spiritual Laws of Success: A Practical Guide to the Fulfillment of Your Dreams*, Deepak Chopra writes, "When you discover your essential nature and know who you really are, *in that knowing itself* is the ability to fulfill any dream you have, because you are the eternal possibility, the immeasurable potential of all that was, is, and will be." Greatness is not your destiny; it is something you always have within you. Reaching that realization is when you'll truly feel fulfilled.

Sabotage

Fears or phobias can hold us back from developing our greatness. Often, we are afraid of the opposition we encounter externally or internally; this resistance can be both real and imagined. We feel threatened by forces we don't see or expect, which causes us to be apprehensive and can hinder our process. As Marianne Williamson put it in her book *A Return to Love: Reflections on the Principles of a Course in Miracles*, "Our deepest fear is not that we are inadequate. Our deepest fear is that we are powerful beyond measure. It is our light, not our darkness, that most frightens us."

Unfortunately, there are many people who sabotage our light, be it intentionally or unintentionally, and we start doubting our path or our beliefs. We experience a lack of support that can cripple us. We can't control other people, or the way they act or react to us. What we do have control over is how we respond to them. By staying true to your goals, you'll be better equipped to handle any outside influences.

I once had a young client with a very promising collegiate career. He was progressing wonderfully through his first two years, until he lost confidence in his lacrosse game. He wasn't shooting for goals anymore and was afraid to catch the ball for fear he would miss and let people down. This lack of confidence spread over into his academics until his grades went from straight As to Ds. His parents were concerned drugs or alcohol were causing a problem, but wanted to try one last effort by using intuitive coaching and hypnosis.

By the time he came to me, he seemed a shriveled version of the boy I had previously known. He was shy, when before he had been outgoing. He was quiet, when previously he was the life of the party. He told me he earlier had a big hit to his ego; his coach told him not to get too confident, that he wouldn't amount to anything, and he decided in that moment that there was no point in attempting to accomplish anything anymore. He felt there was no triumph in him, and no matter how hard he tried he wouldn't be successful in life. His outlook had shifted, and we needed to get him back to feeling he was worthy of greatness.

He needed a little nudge to regain his course. It didn't mean he had to change direction completely in order to get back in his zone; it just meant we needed to encourage the greatness that was within him to show itself again. He had so much promise but couldn't find it anymore. So, we did a bit of intuitive coaching along with hypnosis directed toward increasing his self-esteem, and his confidence began building up again.

Once that started, he was once again able to reclaim his place on his team and in the classroom. He brought his grades back up; he rekindled his desire for lacrosse; and he recouped the friendships he had been lacking. He had not been abusing drugs or alcohol. However, the lack of confidence he had begun experiencing in his sports had overwhelmed him and had dragged him down in every aspect of his life. After I worked with him for just a couple of weeks, he was able to recover his journey toward success. He felt capable of greatness; his light, which he had been slowly extinguishing, was reignited. He was content, and because of that he went on to become captain of his lacrosse team.

You may find that fulfillment is right at your fingertips, but it eludes you, and you're having a difficult time grasping it. This is merely because as we grow our desires change or expand, and what we originally set out to accomplish or attain does not satisfy us as we expected. Fulfillment does not come on a conscious level; it is natural, a subconscious building upon previous growth. It is an ever-changing evolution of ideas, core values, and joy. Above all, fulfillment is experienced as a satisfaction with life and a belief in one's self. When you reach that, there is no greater feeling!

• •
WEEK 6 EXERCISE:
WHAT MAKES YOU HAPPY?

Write the header "What Makes Me Happy!" in your journal. Now's your chance to explore what you believe is necessary and paramount to have, attain, or accomplish in order to have your greatness shine.

Make a list of things you feel you need to have in order to feel fulfilled. This list can include material things, but be sure to list accomplishments and traits you believe will have a personal and positive influence on you. Love, family, career, finances, athleticism, homes, friends, and education are just some of the topics you need to include.

Over the next week, go back and list each item, but include how much of each item you would need to be fulfilled. For example, if money is on your list, write down how much money is necessary per week, per month, or per year.

Now, and this is the hardest part, are you being honest with yourself? Review your list again. If you wrote $1,000 per week, is that enough? If not, correct your answer! This is your fulfillment diary, no one else's. Have the confidence to be true to yourself!

You might find as the week progresses that your ideas have shifted. You may have originally recorded $1,000 per week, but now you realize you need a minimum of $2,500 per week to meet your current bills. Put some thought into what is integral in feeling supported and fulfilled. Do you deserve it? If so, great! If not, why not? List every reason you believe you are not worthy. Is it something you can change? Do you want to change it?

At the end of the week, review what you've written. Summarize in one section what you've decided is fundamental to feeling great. Is everything on your list still important? If you had everything you've recorded, do you think that would fulfill you? Would it make you happy?

Encourage yourself, as you would anyone else, to weed out what would cause you more angst than happiness. Remove anything you originally included to make anyone else happy.

This is for you, no one else. And, again, review it. Are the remaining items causing a stir in your belly? Do they make you excited? Do they feel good?

You are the key to your own fulfillment! Don't sell yourself short. You deserve this!

Manifesting

This week, follow your bliss! Go out and do something that makes you really happy! Will you go dancing, or to an amusement park, or walk through the woods hand in hand with your partner, or sign up for classes to start you on your new path toward manifesting greatness? Decide on something that causes you extreme delight and put it into action!

• •

Chapter 2

Energy

(WEEKS 7–11)

What Is Energy?

Have you ever had a tingling sensation or goose bumps? Yes, it can be a physical occurrence; your foot fell asleep or you're just cold. But, other times, most other times, your hair is standing on end because of energy. Occasionally, you may even feel the crackle of electricity in the room. This is energy—psychic energy and even telekinetic energy carry currents of thought, movement, and connectivity that unite every living creature on the planet. We are all one being, one unit, and we are joined together to help each other succeed, heal, understand, and love.

Energy is transmitted with every thought, feeling, word (said aloud or in your mind), and action. Your spiritual energy is similar to the electrical energy that runs your home. It is charged with positive and negative. It can send shockwaves out or take a charge internally. It is based on a circuit, a balance of push and pull. Everything we feel about ourselves and others goes out into the universe as energy.

There is an old proverb that quite succinctly speaks to the use of our positive and negative energy: "An old Cherokee told his grandson,

'My son, there's a battle between two wolves inside us all. One is Evil. It's anger, jealousy, greed, resentment, inferiority, lies, and ego. The other is Good. It's joy, peace, love, hope, humility, kindness, and truth.' The boy thought about it and asked, 'Grandfather, which wolf wins?' The old man quietly replied, 'The one you feed.'" It's up to us to decide what psychic polarity, positive or negative, we choose to nourish.

We all have an energy field that emanates from our bodies, usually extending out about an inch or two, that is known as our aura (see the "Auras and Chakras" section later in this chapter). Our energetic field runs through us and all around us. It reaches out into the universe and hangs closely by our side. We possess an incredible gift; we are able to tap into this energy and change things in our lives. In reality, we have a responsibility to use this energy, our energy, so it doesn't go to waste!

Shocking energy

Our energy is our power, the place where everything creates. It is this energy we tune in to when we are utilizing our psychic gifts and when we manifest for ourselves, be it positive or negative. This energy, through our gentle or firm direction, creates our success and by extension our greatness. As author Michelle Belanger put it, "In order to live up to your greatest potential as a whole and complete being, you must become aware of this subtle aspect of yourself that is so often ignored in favor of the physical part of your being."

We gather strength through this continuous ethereal stream. In addition to the ability we possess to call up our own energy, we are able to tap into the energetic power of the earth and the universe to connect to our intuition and our consciousness. By channeling this energy, you can heal yourself and others as well. This is the basic premise for Reiki and other hands-on healing methods.

Everyone has a different energy pattern. Some utilize their energy more efficiently, in that they aren't depleted, and others tend to overexpose themselves, draining their energy. We can easily feel the energy of others once we learn to tune in to it. We can also sense where there may be physical issues for ourselves or others, depending on whether our energy field seems to kind of cave in.

During a reading with a client, I did a quick scan of her body. Amanda had asked if I picked up on anything to do with her health. I immediately sensed a general achiness and overall exhaustion from some kind of disease, as well as a collapsed-energy section around her lower leg and ankle area.

She said, "Wow. I have a multitude of autoimmune diseases, and I recently had surgery and therapy on my ankle! It's amazing how you picked up on that!"

I replied, "It's all in your energy field. I can psychically feel where your energy is off. It feels like there are roadblocks up and voids in the space where it should be extending."

By using these visuals, she was able to understand what I was talking about. It was obvious to me I had picked up on the diseases through her blocked energy patterns, and the ankle injury had come through as missing energy. Medical intuitives are able to access the energetic fields of their clients' anatomy in much the same way in order to heal them or help them to heal themselves. Caroline Myss is a well-known author and medical intuitive. According to Caroline in her book *Anatomy of the Spirit*, "This means that I use my intuitive ability to help people understand the emotional, psychological, and spiritual energy that lies at the root of their illness, disease, or life crisis."

No, I don't have bugs

I regularly experience energy in an unusual way. A funny thing happens to me when I do readings. I connect to the other side, and it usually makes my head itch. I can feel a tingling running along my scalp. Imagine goose bumps on steroids on the top of your head. This is pretty much what it feels like, and it makes me scratch at my hair.

If you've ever seen a picture of me, you know I have a lot of hair; it can be quite a sight!

Almost every psychic takes a couple of minutes at the beginning of each session to explain their process to their client. During one of these times, I realized my client was moving away from me, and not in a good way. I finally understood that she wasn't afraid of me; she was afraid of whatever bugs I had in my hair! From that moment on, I've explained during my spiel to my clients that the intuitive energy that's coming through makes my head tingle. Nothing will jump on them, except possibly spirit!

Even though I can create quite the spectacle of myself, I'm glad it happens. It's one of the ways I become aware that spirit is trying to send me information, and that I'm connecting to the universal energy that carries psychic messages to me. This is a clue that I'm tuning in to the other side and that my helpers are ready to go. I love this energetic process!

Just like electrical energy that can shock you, psychic energy also carries with it a charge. If you've ever seen a ghost-hunting show, you've seen the electromagnetic field or EMF detectors they use. That's because ghost or spirit energy can affect the magnetic or energetic field as it materializes. We also have this energy, and we can train it or learn to adapt it to assist us in any situation we desire—connecting to our intuition, the other side, or even manifesting greatness.

· ·

WEEK 7 EXERCISE:

TAPPING INTO YOUR ENERGY

On the first day, it's time to tap into the energy of the earth. It is an incredibly strong and powerful energy that we are able to channel and utilize to our benefit.

Sit in a comfortable chair and plant your feet firmly on the floor. Close your eyes. Visualize roots coming out of the bottom of your feet, reaching all the way down into the center of the earth. Now, feel those roots attaching to the interior core of the earth, growing and spreading around it.

Imagine the energy of the earth rising up through the soles of your feet. As it does, you begin to feel a tingling. Allow the earth's beautiful red and brown energy to travel up your legs, through your knees, into your thighs, and through your hips and reproductive area. As this incredible earth energy travels, allow anything that doesn't feel right or no longer belongs in your body to fall away, down to the earth to be recycled.

Continue with the earth's red and brown energy and let it move up through your abdomen and upward, still, through your chest and heart area. Again, feel the tingle of the earth's grounding energy and allow the psychic and physical debris to fall out of and off of your body to the ground. Let go of whatever no longer serves you.

Imagine the earth's energy moving up even further, into your neck and shoulders, your jaw and your face, through the top of your head. As it does, imagine a waterfall of red and brown energy spilling out of the crown of your head, clearing any leftover debris that is no longer necessary for you to carry.

Sit with this waterfall flowing out for at least five minutes, and breathe deeply. When you are ready, open your eyes, contentedly, knowing you have just cleansed your body, mind, and spirit.

The next day, it's time to bring the spiritual or universal energy to you. Again, go somewhere quiet, where you aren't likely to be interrupted, and sit down, comfortably, without crossing your legs or arms.

Take a few deep breaths and imagine the top of your head. Focus in on how your scalp feels, and your skull underneath that. Take another deep breath and imagine right in the center of the uppermost part of your head a cone shape is beginning to form, its tip extending inside you. Visualize it, a funnel of energy as it spins gently, rising up, moving outward and getting larger. Imagine it is silver, with strings of violet, and that it's growing even bigger, opening up toward heaven.

As it expands, spreading wider, state the intention by saying in your mind, "Please flow all positive energy and information to me, and through me, and assist me in accepting all messages and healing for myself and to share with others." Repeat this over and over until you feel the tingling energetic flow pouring into the funnel and, by extension, into your body.

Feel this beautiful silver and violet energy flow down through your face, your neck and shoulders, through your arms, and all the way until it streams out of your fingertips. Spread it down, through your chest, and abdomen, all the while pushing out any negative energy that no longer belongs there. Continue down through your reproductive organs and your hips, your thighs, and knees, letting this silver healing energy clear out any pain or old debris that no longer belongs there. Bring the energy down through your calves and your ankles and all the way out of your feet and the tips of your toes.

Now, ask for a message. In your mind, say, "What can I hope for; how can I define my greatness?" Wait until you receive an answer. It may be vague or it may be extremely detailed. Either way, process it and remember it, as you will be writing it down. When you're ready, open your eyes, feeling freer and refreshed and excited to be alive.

On day three, you are going to capture your energy so you can be aware of what it feels like to hold it in your hands. Stand with your feet firmly planted on the ground, absorbing the energy from the earth. Close your eyes and just breathe. Focus on your breath as you inhale and exhale.

Slowly, with your hands slightly cupped and your arms comfortably in front of you, chest height, bring your hands together, without touching, imagining you are holding a ping pong ball between them. Begin to feel the ping pong ball, the roundness of it, the warmth of it. This is your energy, your life force, and you may notice a buzzing or a change in temperature as you tune in to it. Stay with this, moving your hands around the imaginary ping pong ball, spreading them apart and bringing them back together.

Then, gradually pull your hands apart until you have an energy baseball in the middle of them. Again, feel the shape. Continue moving your hands around, separating and then coming back, stopping when you feel the energy ball between them.

Make it bigger. Imagine your energy has expanded to the size of a softball now. Continue stretching and pulling the energy around and notice how your hands feel. Do they feel different? Do they feel warmer? Colder? Try and focus on the energy growing larger as you pulse your hands around it. Continue this process at least as long as it takes to really feel the energy buzzing between your hands.

On the fourth day, it's time to enlist some help. Grab a friend! Stand facing your friend. Each of you should hold both hands out in front of you, palms facing each other but not touching. Gently, move your hands toward and away from each other, following your partner's hands. Notice if you feel like there is something between your hands when they are an inch or two apart. If so, great! Move them even farther apart, noticing how far away they are while still feeling the energy. If not, keep trying. Close your eyes and have your partner move their hands. See if you can tell when they are moving them.

On the fifth day, it's time to scan your body like a medical intuitive. Start at the bottom and use your hands to see if you feel any energy, warmth, or lack thereof emanating from your feet and work all the way to the top of your head. Did you notice anywhere on your body that was stronger? Weaker? Void of energy? In any areas that were lacking, have you been experiencing any physical pain or issues? Do it a couple of times slowly, until you're sure of any abnormalities in your energy. Remember, this doesn't mean you have a disease or a tumor! No need to run to the doctor unless you are experiencing other symptoms.

Grab that friend again, or a new one, on the sixth day. It's time to work with a partner. Don't tell each other anything about any ailments or aches and pains you may be having or any surgeries you've had or pre-existing conditions that may be present. Take turns scanning each other's energy and see what you get. Chances are you'll connect!

On the final day this week, relax. Play back in your mind all of the energy exercises you've done. Do the two meditations from the beginning of the week if you want; this can help you recharge your energy. You are an energetic being—enjoy it!

Manifesting

Go outside and hug a tree, literally. Or dig your hands in the dirt of a houseplant without disrupting its roots. Alternatively, just enjoy the outdoors and be with nature in some way. Feel the energy of the universe as it surrounds you. "There is powerful energy running through me and around me."

What Happens with Negative Energy?

Just like an electrical circuit, you have both positive and negative energy. Negative energy can get trapped within our bodies, leaving us feeling lethargic or less than whole. If we continue operating within the negative energy, we will eventually be miserable. We're not made that way, but so often we get stuck there. As author Ted Andrews puts it in his book *The Healer's Manual*, "Our body is an energy resonator and monitor. It has the capacity to resonate with almost any form of energy—positive or negative." We will resonate with both. It is up to us to choose what we hold on to.

Afraid of the dark

Rooms hold energy. They can hold both positive and negative energy. Have you ever walked into a room and felt immediately or even gradually ill? For no apparent reason, you just felt sick? It's quite possible that someone or something was in that room that held a negative vibration. It could have been that there was a fight there or that someone who had a nasty temperament recently left. Or you may find when you go to a restaurant, you ask to be seated somewhere other than where the hostess wants to put you, as I often do. It just doesn't feel right for some reason.

Clearing that energy, specifically if it's somewhere you will be located, can be the best cure for what's ailing you. That's where the Native American or Shaman tradition of smudging can help. Smudging is the process of burning sage and coaxing the smoke throughout the corners and the entrances of a room with the intention of clearing any negative energy that's trapped or left over. You can also smudge yourself, ridding you of any negative energy that you've taken on, due to your own actions or the energetic dumping by others.

Leave me be

Negative energy can get trapped in your joints as well. It often causes pain in your knees, your wrists, your back, or your neck. Have you ever said, "Get off my back!" or "You're a pain in the neck!" It's not because someone is literally climbing on you like a monkey. Instead, they are directing negative energy toward you, and it weighs you down the same as it would if someone jumped on you. Leaving this residual negativity can manifest itself into pain or disease.

Bodily functions can be disrupted by negativity. This type of energy is draining to the physical as well as the spiritual body and can cause feelings of depression or anger, changing the way you view yourself and those around you. Negative energy can also cause anger or resentment or just sheer nastiness. It has the capacity to create a feeling that nothing is going right, that everything is wrong with the world, and, no matter what you do, it won't work out. This happens when there are negative energy blocks in our mental or emotional state. These also need to be cleared, and can be addressed through meditation or spiritual cleansing.

Manifesting happiness is not possible if you are living fully in despair or desperation. Judith Orloff says in her book *Positive Energy: 10 Extraordinary Prescriptions for Transforming Fatigue, Stress, and Fear into Vibrance, Strength, and Love*, "Negative energy keeps us small, unhealthy; it alienates us from our best selves. We may generate it with our own fear, self-loathing, or shame—an emotional terrorism we inflict on ourselves without realizing the toll."

Love and joy cannot exist where negativity resides. When we focus on negative energy, we only have the capability of manifesting things we don't want, or things that are not going to help us. It is impossible to be happy when our thoughts are filled with negativity. Unlike magnetism, where opposites attract, when manifesting, like creates like, so negative vibes will bring negative results. This type of energy is bred from fear, and trying to build from a place of apprehension will never produce positive results.

It's difficult to keep clear from negativity if you are psychically sensitive to others' energy fields. It's very easy to absorb the trauma or drama seeping off of people close to you or even globally, especially if you are empathic or you intuitively feel a person's energy. Learning to protect yourself psychically can aid you in regaining balance and help you from assimilating their problems as your own.

9/11

Immediately before, during, and after the 9/11 terrorist attacks in the United States, scores of people felt the terror and the pain experienced by the families of those lost in the acts of violence that claimed thousands of lives. Obviously, this monumental event carried an overwhelming amount of negative energy. Many psychics, intuitives, and empaths were able to feel the energy shift before the actual attacks took place, and said as much beforehand, but weren't necessarily able to determine exactly what was about to take place. The unnecessary suffering caused by the people involved is still felt to this day, over a decade later, though many try and dissipate it with positive energy and happy memories of lives before the atrocities. It's not that the pain of losing so many has gone away; it's that we are able to focus more on the positive energy they left behind. This makes it just a little bit easier to get on with life.

As I've described, events hold energy—even events that haven't taken place yet. I often do psychic parties. This means I will go to someone's residence and do private fifteen-minute sessions for people. I booked one of these sessions recently, through emails back and forth. I told my husband I just wasn't feeling it. Something about it was off. It wasn't going to happen the way everyone planned it out. I couldn't quite pinpoint why, but I knew I didn't want to go there. The person who was having it was very nice, nothing to worry about with her, and

I wasn't getting anything bad about the guests' vibes. I just knew it wasn't going to work out. Sure enough, we had a snow and ice storm! We had to postpone it. I felt as if a weight had been lifted. Even though it wasn't necessarily a negative event, it felt negative to me. Upon rescheduling, it was fine. No more bad vibes.

Debbie Downer

We've all experienced a "Debbie Downer." This is someone who has the unnerving ability to bring a great mood down, and to swing your optimism to pessimism. These people are known as *psychic vampires*, or *energy vampires*. They seem to suck the life right out of you with all of their negativity. This can happen with strangers or even close friends and relatives.

A few years back, I was having a great day working at a holistic health fair at a local university. I was offering individual sessions to people: healing, psychic, intuitive counseling—whatever they preferred. And then it happened. I was as happy as could be, until "she" sat down in my chair. Immediately, I could feel her bad vibes streaming toward me; she was sending them out in waves. I knew right then: it wasn't going to matter what I said. She had already decided I was no good, would have all the wrong answers, and would come way short of fulfilling her needs. Sure enough, no matter what I said, I was wrong. She made sure that's exactly what happened, and there was no way to make it work for her. So, I just protected myself from her negativity and didn't let it get to me. Feeling this energy from the very beginning helped me to project my positive energy outward to try and cancel out her negative vibes!

Negative energy does not need to stay negative. It can be shifted back to positive, but it's usually up to you to make that adjustment. Once you do, you'll feel the cloud lift. The heavens won't quite open up, and you may not hear choirs of angels sing, but you will feel lighter, freer, and more alive. All that's needed is a shift.

. . . .

The best way to protect yourself from negative energy is to not let it get in. On the first day you are going to do a protective meditation that will keep negativity at bay in even the worst of circumstances.

Close your eyes and breathe. Think of a symbol, something that means happiness to you. It can be a flower, a smiley face, a laughing child, or something else. (But don't use a real child or the image of your own child.) Really think about this, because you will be using it from now on. Then, focus on it. Visualize it clearly—every color, every line, every detail.

Now, relax and take a deep breath. As you inhale, allow positive energy to rise up through your feet from the earth and move all the way up your body and out your fingertips. Exhale out any negativity that you may be experiencing.

As you feel the energy traveling through your fingertips, imagine your happy symbol in your hand as you psychically extend your arm straight out in front of you. Now, with every breath, imagine that symbol duplicating, in a perfect circle, all around your body. Once you've surrounded yourself, imagine pushing the symbols out even farther, and farther still, until you feel totally protected from any negative forces breaking through your happy barrier.

You are now secure and content in your happy place, where nothing can disturb you or bring you down. When you feel totally safe, you can open your eyes. This may take five minutes or it may take an hour. Remember, this is for you, and only you. No one else will experience exactly the same thing!

Over the next couple of days, practice your protective meditation until it feels totally natural. You may find that the symbol you originally thought was perfect for your happiness has changed to something different. That's okay; go ahead and change it.

On the fourth day, you're going to practice some medical intuition to ease any pain you may have been experiencing. Get comfortable and, once again, invoke your protection through your meditation. Then, begin to focus on one or two areas of your physical body where you've been experiencing any type of pain. Imagine your happy symbol, now, moving into that area. You may notice that you feel the discomfort flare as you do this. This is because you are pinpointing that spot. If this happens, great! It means your energy is merging with the ache.

Now, imagine your symbol for happiness is literally pushing outward, clearing the negativity that is trapped in your body causing you soreness. You may feel a change in temperature as the discomfort begins to dissipate. It might feel effervescent even. This is wonderful. You are clearing your pain! Take as long as you need to finish. After you focus on relieving one area, you can take a deep breath and open your eyes, knowing you've done something magnificent for yourself!

On the fifth day, do it again. This time pick a different ache you may have and go after that with your happy symbol. Remember, you have to really visualize it expelling the pain, leaving no room for anything but your happiness.

On the sixth day, get some dried white sage. You can buy it loose or bound, and will find it in many stores, including holistic and whole food stores as well as some bookstores and even grocery stores.

Take it to your home. With some type of shell or ashtray underneath, light the sage and blow the smoke into all of the corners of any room you feel needs cleansing or clearing of negativity. As you do, visualize in your mind that with the smoke of the sage comes light that will push out any negative emotions or energy that's stuck there. Also, be sure to sage around the windows and doorways. Continue through the entire house if you want, visualizing the light that's coming from the smoke, dispersing anything you no longer need.

Finally, on the last day of the week, share your sage with someone you feel may benefit from a clearing. Go to their house or wherever they want to go and cleanse the space and each other. Have your friend stand with their arms extending out from their sides, and blow the sage smoke or use a large feather to fan the smoke around every bit of your friend. Then switch. As your partner is clearing you, imagine that happy symbol spreading all the way around you, again, expelling any negative energy that may be trapped within your physical body and your energetic body.

Remember, if you can't imagine or visualize your happy symbol, you can't create or manifest happiness for yourself. Celebrate your cleansing!

Manifesting

"Negative energy rolls off of me back down into the earth to be recycled into positive energy."

. . . .

Why Be Positive?

Have you ever felt happy and didn't know why? Or have you ever heard the phrase "There's excitement in the air"? That's positive energy. It's palpable energy that you can feel, a current that can create joy seemingly out of nowhere. This positivity has the power to lift you up and raise your spirits, and may even cause bouts of laughter and joviality.

Seeing the light

Negative energy keeps you trapped in "I can't," whereas positive energy brings you to a place of "I can." It's this positive energy that allows forward progression to occur. When you're in this flow, it feels like the universe is able to bless you with many gifts to help you move onward and upward, allowing mobility and natural, positive evolution to continue. In this state, we recognize that the universe can be very generous.

Sometimes we sabotage our own well-being. What we think creates the world around us. Simply stated, every thought we have and every word we speak is energy that we expel into the world. When we send out positive vibes, we attract positivity. That's why it is so important to spread positive energy.

Unless you're a natural empath, most fears are learned. Empaths feel the energy around them. This can be a burden or a blessing. If you are an empath, I'm pretty sure you'd rather soak up the sunshiny feelings of someone who is happy and vibrant than someone who is angry or miserable. Unless you're a glutton for punishment, attracting positive vibes will most assuredly make you feel better. Knowing what that energy feels like will make you crave it even more and helps keep you positive.

Change it up

Getting to that optimistic place is easy when you live with love as your base. When you let fear, instead, decide your path, you will be left with pessimistic energy. The good news is you're able to change your direction in life. You don't have to stay stuck; destiny is yours to make. As the character Princess Merida (voiced by Kelly Macdonald) says in the 2012 computer-animated movie *Brave*: "There are those who say fate is something beyond our command. That destiny is not our own. But I know better. Our fate lives within us. You only have to be brave enough to see it."

There is a misguided belief about those who are spiritual or who are striving to evolve. We, like everyone else, also struggle with fear and inconsistencies. It would be nice to say we didn't, but I'm here to tell you that we absolutely do. Years ago, I realized I was living my life out of fear. Every decision I made was born from fear, rather than love. This caused great distress within my body. The autoimmune diseases were on an upward spiral, in a bad way, and my family felt my angst. Though I was never clinically depressed or anxiety ridden, I was certainly apprehensive. Most of this had to do with finances.

I grew up with my mom, a brilliant and kind woman. She was my best friend and confidant, but she was also a single mother who struggled every day to provide food for three children and a roof over our heads. She didn't tell the landlord if there was a problem because she was afraid of being kicked out for complaining, and though she was very prideful, she let society dictate what she could have and who she was allowed to be. This she did out of fear: fear for her children and what our lives would become.

I looked up to my mom; her courage and her struggles made her the woman she was, but they also depleted her life force until she had nothing left to fight for. I learned from her not to speak out if there was a chance it could come back against me, and to live from a place of "If I do this, then what will happen with that?" It took me many years to decide I wasn't going to live from this place anymore. I understood it was time to stop giving away my power.

On a New Year's Day, quite a while ago, I changed my life. I gave my worries up to the universe and swore I would no longer come from a negative platform regarding money and opportunities, and instead be positive. I had my own intention ceremony at a brook nearby, and into the brook I threw a stick for everything I was ready to be rid of. There was one stick for fear of money, one for allowing panic to ruin my day, one for negative emotions, one for reacting to things out of apprehension, and so on. This has changed my life. Fear is not the boss of me. I have my power back and I'm never giving it away again!

Making that change to positivity allowed me to step into my power. I am now able to fully realize my potential and recognize the positive vibes I can spread to the universe. I've also come to feel a karmic balance in the universe; the more affirmative energy I send out, the more positive energy bounces back to me.

. . . .

WEEK 9 EXERCISE:
SIMPLY POSITIVE

It's time to break the trance that's held you in the negative. You are a spiritual being, and as such you deserve to be happy! On the first day you are going to send yourself positive, healing heart energy.

Get a bowl of water and put it down next to you. In a comfortable and quiet setting, begin by breathing. Take in positive, healing breaths and breathe out negative, angry breaths. Place your right hand in the bowl of water and your left hand over your heart.

Pay attention to your heart. As you continue your breathing, imagine feeling a bright stream of energy flowing through your left hand directly into your heart. Then, with every beat of your heart, visualize any negativity traveling out of your heart, pumping through your bloodstream until it gets to the tips of your right hand and pours into the water.

Continue doing this until you feel all of the negativity has been dispersed out, into the bowl. You may notice after you're all done that the water has, incredibly, turned cloudy or has become darker or even dirty-looking!

On the next day, you're going shopping! You don't have to spend any money, but you do have to hit up a nearby mall. Before going inside, set your intention that your protective bubble will surround you. This can help keep you from experiencing any overwhelming feelings if you're an empath or of being bombarded by external energy due to crowds.

Now, go into each store, briefly, and be still. Don't focus on what actual store it is, just go through the entry. Feel what the energy feels like. Does it feel good? Does it feel bad? Is it hard to breathe? Is it relaxing? Do you want to stay? Do you want to leave? Pay attention to how your body feels.

Finally, which stores did you feel positive in? Which did you feel negative in? Are you able to recognize the difference?

On the third day, try this with people. Write down a list of people you associate with. Be sure to include friends, coworkers, family, and others you interact with regularly. Now, make sure these people don't see your list—you are not trying to start anything negative with them!

One by one, begin by focusing on the person's name. Then, visualize them. Pay attention to how your body feels, how your spirit feels. Do they feel good? Do they feel yucky? Give each person at least three to four minutes of your time. Write down a "P" or "N" next to each name, for positive or negative, depending on how you react.

After you're all done, go back. Does it feel right? Does it match how you feel toward the person in general? If you've written an "N" next to a name, will you address it? Will you back away from that person or make an effort to change how you interact?

On the fourth day, do the first exercise again. You need to be sure to recharge your batteries with positivity so you don't start attracting negativity!

On the fifth day, it's time to get physical. Exercise clears your body of psychic and physical debris. It contributes to your well-being, in every possible way. Whether you regularly exercise or not, you will start today! Depending upon your level of previous activity, you can take it very easy, from Pilates-type exercise if you're lying in bed, to yoga, and all the way up to running ten miles. The type of exercise you do is up to you.

Before you start, tune in to your body. Do you feel tired? Sluggish? Achy? Uncomfortable? This is all going to change. Now, exercise! Do whatever works for you. Make sure you stretch your body out before you begin and stretch your body out after. Walk, do yoga, lift weights, run, dance; it's all good!

Now, how do you feel? You may feel tired from working out, but it'll be a great kind of tired! You should be experiencing positive energy right now. Write the results in your journal.

On the sixth and seventh days, make it your mission to only allow positivity to linger in your energy. Go about your days—work, read, and play. If at any point during these two days it feels like negativity may be creeping in, imagine sparkly, effervescent, shiny squiggles of light coming in and pushing out any dark or yucky energy. It may feel tickly—great! Smile! Smiling helps combat any of those depleting or defeating energies. Take it to another level and laugh. Laugh, laugh, laugh! This clears out and cleanses your spirit by expelling negative vibes. Grab a friend, and laugh with them!

Manifesting

"I send out positive energy, and I receive positive energy as well."

. . . .

Auras and Chakras

Most people have seen or experienced the human aura, though they may not have recognized it. The aura is an energy field that surrounds every living thing. It is sometimes identified as a pure white light and other times seen clearly as colors. This aura projects our energy into the world and can be as tight as an inch from the physical body to, in extremely rare cases, miles away.

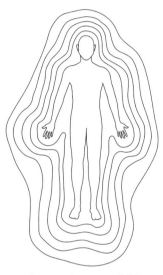

Our auric energy field

Aura you good?

All auras are different, depending on the person and also the moment, as auras change constantly. These energy fields contain information about us—physical, emotional, and spiritual data that can be used to help us heal. External energy can negatively affect your aura, especially if it is weak or damaged by illness or low self-esteem. On the flip side, it can also positively influence your mood, especially if your aura is strong and fortified.

When we work on manifesting, our desires are sent out via our auric energy into the universe. If we have a cleansed and healthy aura, our wishes are more likely to be attained. If our aura is filled with pockets of ill will or deceit or despair, the chances of manifesting what we truly desire become lessened, as does our ability to manifest greatness. Greatness will come, but only when our aura is, for the most part, strong.

. . . .

WEEK 10 EXERCISE:

AURAS

This week you will tune in to your own and others' auras. You will learn what the aura feels like, how it appears, and how it changes.

On the first day, you will try and see your own aura. Some people find it's very effortless to see an aura, while others struggle to get even a glimpse. Luckily, the more you practice, the easier it is.

Place your hand about a foot in front of your face. Try and situate it in front of a plain white background. Just stare at the space between your fingers. As you look, allow your eyes to blur a bit. Then, move your hand to about two inches in front of your face. At both distances, notice if you see any shadows or colors between your fingers. If not, do you feel any colors? If you don't, imagine you do. What color(s) are there? Keep doing this for at least half an hour, shifting your hand in and out. Do you see any energy there?

On the next day, use a mirror to view the space around your head. Sit comfortably and do the same thing you did with your hand, but this time go even farther away from the mirror. Continue looking about one to three inches above and around your hair, and notice if you see or feel any light or color.

Grab a friend on the third day! Take turns standing in front of a white wall. Start with your friend facing you and try and see their aura. If you don't see it, can you feel it? You may notice areas appear different—possibly brighter or lighter, fuller or less pronounced. Have your friend turn and face the wall. Do you see their aura now? Can you feel it? Then switch. It's your turn to stand in front of the wall. Does your friend see it? Try and project your energy out farther. Do they see it now?

On the fourth day, go out. Go to the store or, even better, a sports game. Try and focus in on a variety of people. Notice if you see any energy around them. If so, which colors, if any, do you see? Do you feel anything? Continue until you get something, even if it only feels like your imagination. Usually, when watching a game, a fan's aura can be projected pretty strongly as they are experiencing the emotions attached to the game. If possible, try and go to a sporting event, or to a place where others are watching one.

Get a couple of friends together for the next day. Have them sit facing each other, eyes closed. Look at them and feel with your own energy if you perceive their auras. Ask them, one at a time, to project their aura out, toward their partner. If they are up to it, ask them to imagine a very happy thought and project that out. Also, and only if they are both amenable, have them project a very angry thought. Do you feel a difference? Have them switch, taking turns. You can also try it with just one friend. Can you sense their aura?

For the last couple of days, practice all of the exercises, paying special attention to whether there are certain times you are able to see the aura more clearly.

Chakra it up to energy

Chakras, our spiritual energy centers, go together with the aura. They are spinning wheels of energy, our spiritual batteries, which regulate and govern our chi, or life force. They are conduits of universal energy.

There are seven major chakras in our ethereal or spiritual body; each is responsible for controlling different aspects of our life.

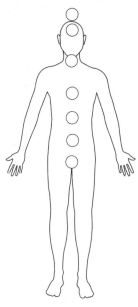

Our chakra system

The lower, or bottom three, chakras have to do with need. They are attached to a physical desire or drive. The first chakra, or *base chakra*, is red. It is located at the base of the spine, under the sexual organs. This root chakra represents your foundation, your security. It's linked to financial and spiritual security. The second chakra, or *sensual chakra*, is orange, and spins about two inches below your bellybutton. This energy relates to our senses as well as our sexuality. It also has a deep connection with our creativity. Located in the solar plexus, the third, or *sacral chakra*, spins yellow and is your power center. It's also responsible for your gut instinct as well as your will and helps you with your psychic sense, clairsentience.

The upper chakras are linked more closely to consciousness as well as spiritual matters. Your fourth, or *heart chakra*, is green. This is the love chakra, the one that spreads compassion and joy as well as healing energy. The fifth, or *throat chakra*, is also related to creativity, and is blue. It is specifically about communication, speaking your truth, listening clairaudiently, sharing messages from the other side, and your intuition. Your *third eye*, or sixth chakra, indigo in color, is your clairvoyant and transcendent chakra. It's what helps you psychically see and guides your imagination. And, finally, your *crown chakra*, violet in color, connects you to the universal energy, opening your psychic ability and connecting you to the Divine. This spiritual chakra is at the very top of your head and is your connection to intuition and claircognizance, or psychic knowing.

Your aura and chakras are connected energetically. The aura holds a wealth of knowledge that radiates through and from the chakra system. Within the aura, you can psychically sense if any of the chakras are off or unbalanced. These chakras spin, like little wheels, and if they are not spinning properly, it can cause disruptions in your energy field that can indicate things like illness, disease, anger, and even mood swings. Making the connection between your aura and chakra system as clean and pure as possible lends itself to manifesting greatness.

• •

WEEK 11 EXERCISE:

CHAKRAS

Though chakras and auras have to do with your energy and can show up as colors, they are two distinctly different parts that contribute to your energetic body. This is why it's important to take the time to stimulate and work with both.

For your first exercise, it's time to open up your chakras. Be somewhere quiet and comfortable. You can sit or lie down, but be sure you won't be disturbed.

Imagine your feet are submerged in a small warm-water spring that's bubbling with the energy of the earth. Feel that energy as it rises up through your toes, your heels, and your ankles, and farther up your shins and your knees and your thighs.

As the bubbling energy moves up to your first chakra, between your legs, imagine a spinning red pinwheel. See the deep red color and feel the bubbling energy as it spins, ridding this root chakra of any psychic debris that no longer belongs there. Allow the bubbles to carry away any physical or energetic negativity that doesn't serve you.

Once that chakra is spinning, perfectly balanced, move the bubbles up to your second chakra, an inch or two below your navel. Imagine an orange pinwheel spinning off any sensual or sexual stress you may have experienced. As it does, it frees up your reproductive area to any necessary healing you may need while losing any residual negativity.

As the bubbles move farther up to your solar plexus, allow that yellow pinwheel to spin freely, removing any doubt about your personal power. At the same time, feel your gut instincts opening up.

The effervescent bubbles are traveling into your chest, your heart chakra, now. A beautiful green color is spinning from the fourth chakra, sending positive healing energy to yourself and others while it lets go of any old injuries or traumas.

Now, it's traversing its way up to your throat area. Feel the blue energy center spinning, bringing you clear hearing and the freedom and ability to share your thoughts and ideas with others. The earth's beautiful energy is clearing any blocks that may have been present as this pinwheel balances and rids itself of any negativity.

Moving up to your third eye, an incredible energy can be felt due to the spinning of this indigo-colored chakra. Your psychic vision becomes clearer as your clairvoyant pinwheel spins and becomes more in tune with positive energy.

Finally, the energy of the bubbles is carried up to your crown chakra on the top of your head. This beautiful and spiritual violet pinwheel spins in a rapid and beautifully balanced circle, opening you up to receive guidance and clarity.

Allow the energy of the bubbling earth energy to flow down around you, warming your entire body and filling it with positivity. Stay with this energy until you are ready to open your eyes and move on.

On the second day, you are going to focus on the first and second chakras. Take off your shoes and your socks. Find yourself a really lush patch of grass and walk on it! That's right, just walk! But, as you do, feel every blade under your feet and your toes and allow your senses to open up with each step. (If you can't get outside, or if it's winter, do it inside. Close your eyes and use your imagination to transform your rug into thick, green, fresh, earthy grass.) The earth's energy is rising up and filling your first and second chakras with positive energy, creating a sense of security and stability. As this happens, let yourself experience a feeling of intense sexuality, all of your senses coming alive. Stay on this grass for at least half an hour to truly accept this feeling of security and sexuality.

The following day, it's time to tune in to the third and fourth chakras through laughter. Laughter opens your diaphragm and is healing for you and everyone around you. Lie down and place your left hand on your solar plexus and your right hand on your heart. Begin by smiling. Let that smile get bigger and more expressive. Now, chuckle. That's right, just a little giggle. You may feel your belly moving slightly. Then, laugh. It may not feel right at first, but that's okay. Just keep doing it. Now, really give it your all. Big, giant belly laughter! That kind of guffawing that only happens when you are really happy!

By putting your hand over your solar plexus, you are sending your power, the energy of your third chakra, and sharing it with your healing heart chakra. Enjoy this laughter until you can't laugh anymore! You may find it so overwhelming to really laugh that you start experiencing a release of emotions. This is great! If not, no worries—it will come.

Now it's time to work on your throat and third eye chakras. These psychic communication centers are crying out to be opened. Go somewhere you can be alone. Put on headphones with music playing and close your eyes. (If you don't have headphones, you can also go somewhere in your car, park, lock the doors, and lie back with the music playing.) Sing along to the music, as loud as you want. It doesn't matter if you're off-key or not; no one can hear you. Use that throat chakra with no worries about what you sound like. Do this for at least four songs.

Now, pick music without words. Keeping your eyes closed, visualize what the music says to you. Allow yourself to envision any images that come to mind and focus on them. Are they in black and white? Color? Are there people? Objects? Just shapes or colors? Whatever it is that you see with your eyes closed, go with it. Keep practicing this until you no longer see anything in your mind's eye.

On the fifth day, imagine silver curlicues springing out of the top of your head, reaching and connecting to positive energy. Feel your scalp as it begins to tingle while you watch, clairvoyantly, these swirly silver threads of energy stretching beyond where you can see. Set your intention that you will receive back helpful energy—information that will assist you in your life in some way. Continue this very important psychic search through the universe until either you no longer feel the tingly energy or you become sleepy.

For the sixth and seventh days, practice all of the exercises and notice which feel the most comfortable to you. Be sure to do the chakra meditation to balance your energy each of these days as well.

Manifesting

"I extend my energy all the way out to _____."

· ·

Chapter 3

Identifying Intuition

(WEEKS 12–17)

Opening to Your Intuitive Senses

Everyone is born with some degree of intuition. Sometimes it's as simple as a nagging feeling that you need to go in a certain direction or a feeling in the pit of your stomach that something's wrong. Other times, it's something more developed or advanced like mediumship (talking to the deceased). Being open to the possibility that you have the capacity to tune in can enhance your natural evolutionary process.

Intuition is described as instinctive knowledge—knowing or being aware of something without having any evidence or proof of its existence, or believing something without discovering it or having perceived it in any rational or logical way. By its definition alone, intuition is something that naturally occurs, without evidence or reason, but it's a phenomenon that can be proven.

Developing your greatness is a journey. Everyone's path is different, but for all it is not something simply to arrive at or buy or be gifted with; it's something you bring out in yourself. Along the way, your intuitive senses are there, begging to be utilized and recognized as a means to help you expand your capacity for greatness. But first you have to understand that you do indeed receive psychic impressions every day, in many ways. These gut instincts, most importantly, allow you to glimpse into what your greatness is—they give you insight to your potential and your future as well as your joy.

Pay attention

I've yet to meet someone who hasn't had the "telephone experience." It's so common that it deserves a classification. I am constantly picking up the phone to call my friend Kim, only to receive a text from her before I can do so. Or, I am in the middle of something and all of a sudden have a desire to call her, out of the blue, and she'll message me online. Have you ever had the phone ring while you're thinking of someone or just after you've thought about them, and they are on the other end? Or, even vice versa. You all of a sudden had a feeling you needed to call someone, and when you do they explain they were just thinking of you? This is a psychic connection or an intuitive link that you've shared with that other person.

Have you ever walked into a restaurant where the server brings you to a table but you hesitated to sit down? It's as though you are being prohibited or blocked from that location. You may feel a subconscious tug on your body to go in a different direction or sit somewhere else. That's your intuition—you're feeling discomfort in that space for whatever reason. Listen to it! Or you may be as surprised as my client Rick was.

Many years ago, Rick asked for a different table when he was led by his waitress to a window seat in a small restaurant. She seemed surprised that he wanted to move, as she had directed him to one of the best tables in the café. The friend Rick was with also wanted to stay there, so Rick succumbed. He sat down, but felt on edge as they looked over the menu, deciding what to order. All of a sudden, a waiter who was carrying a tray full of drinks walked by and stumbled, spilling them all over Rick! Luckily, no one was hurt, but that day was a distinct turning point in his life. He decided there was definitely something to intuition, and from then on he was going to listen to his!

And the reason is

Though not everyone will become a professional intuitive or a psychic conduit to the other side, we all have plenty of reasons to use our intuition, including allowing it to help guide us toward manifesting greatness. Paying attention to the subtle, and sometimes not-so-subtle, intuitive nudges or gut instincts can assist us in pursuing a course in life that will be beneficial to us. By channeling this direction, we can begin to create what it is we want out of life, what's important to us.

Think about how often we question which way to go—whether it's driving a car or something more important like what to do with our life. If we listen to our intuition, that quiet voice in our minds or gentle sensation in our bodies, it will feel more right than if we fight it. Imagine swimming in a river; which way is smoother? Flowing downstream with the current is much easier than trying to swim upstream, struggling against the waves. Fighting the natural flow of your sixth sense is the same thing; it will only bring you angst or, at the very least, resistance.

When we are on the right path, our life feels more cohesive, more purposeful. This encourages manifestation for our greatest good. Tuning in to our psychic senses allows us to create what will be best for us. It is part of our spiritual nature to desire greatness, and it is this same spirit that yearns to manifest it. We can choose to manifest something positively—that is, we can make a conscious decision to tap into and create that which we want, or we can get stuck in manifesting something we don't want in an unconscious effort to balance ourselves.

Creation

We create the life we live, and it's our responsibility to change it if we don't like it. By denying the power our intuition has, we unconsciously connect to experiences we don't want to happen. Take, for instance, trips out in public. When was the last time you ran to the grocery store or the pharmacy or even out to get coffee after you just rolled out of bed? You pray you don't run into anyone you know, but what happens? The second you walk through the door, looking like something the cat dragged in, your ex-boyfriend or ex-girlfriend looks right at you and says hello, with a smirk. Great. But that's not all. You continue into the store to get what you want, and you run into the biggest gossip in town. Even better.

This is negative manifestation. You sent out your vibes, but instead of doing it in a positive way, it bounced back in a negative way. You are connected to everything in the universe, intuitively. Thus, you are able to create or manifest through that intuitive link. Stating you don't want something to happen can backfire, which is why it is always a good idea to manifest in the positive. Instead of "I hope I don't run into anyone," it should be "I will happily shop by myself," or something along those lines.

"Believe in yourself! Have faith in your abilities! Without a humble but reasonable confidence in your own powers you cannot be successful or happy," said Norman Vincent Peale. He believed we all have the wherewithal to create a great state of being. Opening to your intuition is the beginning of a whole new aspect of life. What used to seem like an illusion becomes part of your new reality. This reality can and will help you manifest what feels right intuitively.

• •

WEEK 12 EXERCISE:
DO I USE MY INTUITION?

Using your intuition occurs on a daily basis, but we don't always recognize it. It can be as uncomplicated as buying coffee beans because you have a feeling you're out, and having that validated when you grab the empty bag out of the cabinet when you get home, or it can be more significant, like slowing down while driving on the throughway and gliding past the police radar trap around the next bend. The more you develop and use your intuitive senses, the more your intuition will help you create a life you love.

Each day, over the next week, write down at least one way you've tuned in to, purposely or accidently, and used your intuition. Record whether it was significant in any chain of events that occurred before or after listening to your psychic sense. Pay attention to whether you've had more than one intuitive experience daily as the week progresses. Did you have to consciously note when you had a psychic flash? Or did it just feel natural?

On the last day of the week, go over your list and note whether you are surprised by your intuitive connections. Do you think you would have previously recognized each of them as a psychic experience? Are you thinking about them differently now?

Manifesting

"I trust in my intuition."

. . . .

Identifying Your Intuitive Abilities

While we all share a common intuitive ability, we may experience it differently. Some people will see in their mind's eye—a flash of an image or a picture, much like a Polaroid. Others may feel as though they are watching snippets of a movie play out in their mind. This psychic sense is known as *clairvoyance*. Hearing voices inside your head does not (always) mean you're crazy; it can simply be your psychic hearing, or *clairaudience*. When we feel something, or have a gut instinct, we are experiencing *clairsentience*. And *claircognizance* is knowing something without a logical reason. Recognizing the intuitive flashes by using these four basic psychic senses is what separates merely existing from truly living.

Understanding how you tune in is crucial to identifying your psychic spark. Deep down, you've always known what you're more naturally drawn to; it's just a question of confirming for yourself. No one else can really tell you whether you are clairvoyant, clairaudient, clairsentient, or claircognizant. It's going to depend on what feels right, to you and for you. Whether you are just using these tools for yourself or you are practicing to help others professionally, learning what intuitive sense you connect with will help you when manifesting.

. . . .

WEEK 13 EXERCISE:
PROTECTION AND CONNECTION

Each day this week needs to be spent learning to protect yourself and your energy from any unwanted or negative energy. For this exercise, you should wear non-restrictive clothes and sit or lie down in a comfortable spot. Be sure you won't be interrupted for the next five to ten minutes, as you'll want to be able to relax without being disturbed. You can also read the following aloud and tape it, so you can be fully present for the meditation.

In your settled-down state, begin by taking deep breaths. Feel the breath as it goes in and out. When you inhale, focus on positive energy entering your body. When you exhale, allow all negativity to be released. With every breath, you'll find yourself becoming lighter, free from tension, and more centered.

Imagine a circle of white light spreading around you, all around you, at a comfortable distance from your body. As you continue to breathe, the positive energy you inhale charges this circle of white light, while the negativity you exhale passes outside of the sphere, never to be let back in. Notice how your breath works in perfect harmony as the circle pulses larger, giving you a feeling of extended security. Feel the warmth and comfort of the white light as it wraps you like a warm blanket, protecting you, keeping you safe from any negativity.

Now, visualize a beautiful silver thread weaving throughout the white light. This silver thread will connect you to universal knowledge. As long as you continue visualizing this sphere of protection, you will have access to the other side, your guides, the universe, and all other messengers waiting to share relevant stories and information with you.

Now that you're open and ready to receive, ask the universe to allow you to communicate and take in messages. Begin by asking for a guide to show themselves to you. Intuit whatever information you can over the next five minutes about your guide. You may find that you have more than one. Ask for their name or names. See it, hear it, feel it, or just know it. Then say thank you.

Slowly, take a deep breath in, and exhale. Take another deep breath and begin to move your fingers and toes. Inhale again and feel your spirit coming back into your body. When you're ready, open your eyes.

Every day for the rest of the week, practice this meditation. Write down whatever information you receive during each session. Include whether you "met" any of your guides, what they looked like, if they named themselves, if they told you anything else. Also ask them if they have any gifts for you. You may find you are introduced to many different guides or just one, or that you feel mostly connected to deceased loved ones from the other side.

Whatever you experienced, take the last day to summarize how it all felt to try and connect to your higher good, your higher self, and your guides. Did you enjoy it? Did it resonate with you? Do you feel more comfortable in your quest to tap into your intuition? Does it feel like this will make it easier to manifest greatness?

Manifest

"My intuition will help me reach my greatness."

. . . .

Clairvoyance: Look

Many years ago, I was doing a psychic reading. Tammy wanted to know if I saw her writing a book and if it would be successful. She very much wanted to be published, but wasn't sure if it would serve her career enough to make it worth the effort.

"But how do I know? I really want this to happen, but what's the point if it's not going to help my career? Is this just a pipe dream? Should I forget about it?" Tammy asked me.

I could see the look of desire in her eyes. She wanted to write, and write she should!

I told her, "I see you publishing more than one book, and that each subsequent book will help propel you in your profession."

I saw this with clairvoyance. I didn't see the actual name or title of any of the books. What I saw was her sitting at a table, hair up in a loose bun, pencil sticking out of it. I saw her hand holding a pen, scribbling off her signature as a line of people waited, books in hand. I focused in on the first book, and saw no one in line, but I understood this first work would help pave the way for a second, distinctly different-styled book.

"Whoa, hold on!" Tammy countered back. "Why would I even write the first one, then? What's the point if I don't get anything out of it?"

"The point is you will! It won't be a number-one best seller, and it won't even be critical to your career, but it will help your platform as an author," I told her.

I knew without a doubt that although she is a psychotherapist, she also has the heart and soul of an author and teacher.

When I focused on her second book, I saw her traveling the world. I had visions of Tammy getting on planes, and saw her lecturing and teaching from various stages. I saw flags of different countries waving, though I didn't really focus on which countries.

"Okay, but when? When will everything happen? I'm getting old already!" she exclaimed with a tinge of mock desperation.

"Your first one will come in less than two years, and your second will be in soon after that, but with a different publisher, and you will never be old!" I retorted.

"Well, all right. But what will I write about? Will it be my novel?"

"Not yet. Sex sells," I answered, "but sex with a teaching twist."

And, sure enough, she is now a top-selling author and travels the world with her books *Getting the Sex You Want* and *The New Monogamy*, and has more on the way! She was able to use her own visions, coupled with my visions of her success, to begin manifesting her desires by focusing on those images I shared with her.

We don't always see what we expect, but that doesn't mean it's wrong. The translations are important. Not knowing what everything means all the time is all right; we simply have to be open to the clairvoyant visions. There are no limits to what we can manifest when we focus on our psychic visions.

• •

WEEK 14 EXERCISE:

WHICH PSYCHIC SENSE DO I USE?—CLAIRVOYANCE

It's time to practice your clairvoyance. Remember, on every day, to do the circle of protection meditation before you do any of these exercises. On the first day of the week, you'll need some crayons. Get out some basic colors—red, orange, yellow, green, blue, and purple. Hold them and really see what each looks like. Then, put them down and mix them up. Close your eyes and pick up one at a time. Try and see, with your clairvoyant vision, your psychic sense, what color you have in your hand.

Keep going and try to get at least half of them correct. Remember, you're exercising your psychic eyes, to see if your prevalent intuitive sense is clairvoyance. Don't worry if you have a hard time with this or if it seems you get it wrong more than you get it right.

You may not be psychic, but you will play one with the TV! On the second night, turn on the television and put it on mute. With the remote in hand, change the channel, one at a time. Before you hit the button, try and intuit or psychically see with your third eye what will be on the screen. For example, will it be a building? A person? A car? A band? An animal? Outside? Inside? Words? Clairvoyantly see what will appear on the TV when you change the channel, before you view it with your physical eyes. Practice this for as long as you like, but be sure to do it a minimum of ten times.

On the third night, you are going to use ordinary playing cards. Get out a deck and shuffle the cards, number side down. Now, one by one, you are going to turn them over. But before you do, imagine you can psychically see the color of the card before you flip it. Traditionally, the colors will be black and red. Again, do this at least ten times and note how often you get them correct.

Next, intuit each card's suit. Ordinarily, you will have hearts, diamonds, spades, and clubs. Repeat the process, but this time use your clairvoyance to see what group the next card fits into.

Finally, after you've practiced with the color and the suit, it's time to psychically tune in to what number you'll turn over. Use your intuitive sight to foretell the number. Remember, it may also be a letter representing jacks, queens, and kings.

On the next night, you need to work with a friend. Have them bring pictures of different loved ones. They can either be alive or deceased; either way, you're going to be working with their energy. Have your partner hold one picture at a time, without looking at it. Tune in to the picture and note what you see. Tell your friend what color hair, if any, your clairvoyance is showing you. Also, is the person a male or female? Color of clothes? Approximate age, young or old? Is it a solitary portrait or is there a background? What colors are in the pictures? After you've gone through all of the pictures, have your partner pick them one by one and look at them so they can think of the picture and psychically send you the image. Which way works better for you? How accurate have you been?

For the rest of the week, use your clairvoyance to psychically see who's calling you or who's texting you before you actually look at your phone. Also, tap into that sense when you go to the store; do you see anyone you know? Finally, keep practicing all of the exercises, being sure to tune in using only your third eye, or your psychic sight.

Manifesting

Create a vision board. Put pictures, words, and the like on a piece of posterboard that represent your greatness as you see it psychically. Tune in to it! And, then, put it under your bed for the rest of the year. Take it out occasionally when you want to be reminded.

. . . .

Clairaudience: Listen up

Tapping into more than one sense can help us really define what we are hoping to create. When I do readings for people, I am open to all of my psychic senses. This means I have to be alert and ready to see, hear, feel, and know things. I even have to be open to smells (*clairolfaction*) and tastes (*clairgustance*). Often, I'll use them all to help me interpret the messages I'm being given.

It is not always easy to determine what psychic or clear sense is more prevalent for you until you begin recognizing that you are having intuitive flashes or experiences. This is especially true with clairaudience. Seeing a picture flash before your psychic eyes, in your mind, is one thing, but hearing psychically is quite different. It can feel as though you're imagining the whole thing. Somehow, hearing the words feels more made up, more contrived.

This happens to me quite often. I do readings for clients all the time, and I get similar information for many of them. For example, most people are coming in because they want to know about their careers, finances, relationships, family, and health. Because of the common themes, I'll habitually hear the same thing from one client to the next. Words like *divorce, finances, book,* and *purpose* all play a familiar role during the readings. So I find myself questioning whether my clairaudience is really my imagination or my memory from a previous reading. That's when I have to just trust what I'm getting.

I do mediumship as well as psychic readings. This means I talk to dead people. Not that I see them in full color standing behind my client, but I hear them clairaudiently, and see them clairvoyantly, in my mind.

One day I did three readings in a row, which is not unusual. What was interesting about this day was that I kept getting the same initials, and the same names of deceased loved ones, coming through. None of the clients were related or even knew each other, but this didn't matter. Somehow the universe had set it up that "J" or "Joe" was coming through, with "M" or "Mary" in tow. Now, what makes this more fascinating is other names like "H," "Harvey," and "S," "Sallie," were also coming through. While Joe and Mary are common names, Harvey and Sallie are not as common. I had to really check in with my intuition to determine whether these names were for each individual client or just residuals from previous readings!

One evening I was doing a gallery event for about fifteen women, during which I communicated with deceased loved ones with everyone sitting in attendance. After having many people come through, I began hearing the jingle "Trust the Gorton's Fisherman" for Gorton's frozen fish. I also heard George Clooney and Mark Wahlberg's voices talking about "the perfect storm." I couldn't put it all together, and nobody was claiming it as their message, so I moved on to another deceased loved one trying to deliver a message from the other side.

But the jingle kept coming back. I couldn't get it out of my head! Then, when still nobody from the audience was taking credit for this information coming through, I stopped.

"I know it sounds strange, but I can't continue until someone owns it! I'm also getting the name John," I said, laughing, while at the same time very serious. Someone was trying really hard to come through.

Then Sharon walked in from the kitchen. She had been refilling her drink and missed the jingle that I couldn't help but share with everyone ... again and again. Immediately, she began crying.

"Oh, my goodness! That's my Uncle John!" she exclaimed.

"Well, can you explain it? Because I don't get it," I answered. "Though I'm getting that it's kind of a famous event in which many people were never found."

"Well, my uncle was a fisherman—hence the 'Gorton's Fisherman' jingle—out of Massachusetts. And he was captain of a fishing boat that went down, crew and all. They based the movie *The Perfect Storm* on the ship's disappearance. George Clooney and Mark Wahlberg starred in it," she explained, and it all made sense.

I was receiving the information in a way that I could relate to. I heard the jingle and the voices. I'd seen the movie and couldn't help but be touched by it. This was John's way of getting the information to me that I needed in order to pass it on to Sharon.

If I had let it go, and not trusted the nagging feeling that what I was hearing was not merely my imagination, I would never have given Sharon the peace she craved. Passing along this message of the afterlife connection also helped all the others who were there to experience and share in the knowledge that the message was genuine; connecting to the other side is for real. Everyone sat up a little taller after that experience, although their jaws dropped a bit lower to the ground!

That is a perfect example of clairaudience. Recognizing that it was not something I made up allowed me to share the message. While most people will not be talking with dead people, many will experience some form of clairaudience. Often, this intuitive sense stands out and is prevalent for people who normally use their physical hearing, such as musicians and therapists. You don't have to be psychic to hear the voices inside your head!

• •

WEEK 15 EXERCISE:

WHICH PSYCHIC SENSE DO I USE?—CLAIRAUDIENCE

Often, we don't recognize the sounds and noises we hear when tuning in to our clairaudience because we are unable to discern the sounds and noises with our physical hearing sense. For this first day, tune in to and really hear all of the sounds around you. Do you hear your dog snoring? Can you make out the sound of the dragonfly as its wings flutter next to you? How about the water running through the pipes or the cars passing by your home? Can you make out the lyrics to a song on the radio? Or the words muttered over a loudspeaker system in a store or school? Listen to the conversations of others, not for the sake of eavesdropping but to fine-tune the clarity with which you can hear them. If we can't hear what is around us, how can we expect to tune in to a frequency that is on another plane of existence? Practice this for the first day and night.

On the second day of the week, begin invoking your psychic shield by repeating the protection meditation from above. After you've done that, take the same crayons you used for the clairvoyance exercise and place each in your hand, one at a time. As you do, with your eyes open, say the name of the color you're holding. Repeat it ten times. After you've done all of them, put them down and mix them up without looking. Then, again, with your eyes closed, one by one pick them up and listen with your psychic hearing. Try and tune in and listen to the color. You may hear it spelled out, or you may hear the actual color as a word. If you don't hear anything, ask in your mind what shade it is. Keep going, practicing with all the different colors at least ten times. If you still feel like your clear hearing is not working and you're having a hard time tuning in, just imagine you can hear the crayon name. Sometimes, just imagining can actually help you tap into your psychic senses. Keep track of whether or not you are able to hear with your clairaudience any of the crayon colors.

On the third day, psychically listen to the radio. In your car or in your home, practice hearing what song will be playing when you change the station. Will it be someone talking instead? Be sure to try this at least ten times. Remember, there are thousands of songs that could be playing. Even if you get only one right, give yourself kudos!

It's time to meet your guides again, this time with the specific intention that you will hear them. On this fourth day, close your eyes and imagine that your psychic guides are coming to you, wanting to give you information. Begin by asking your guide to tell you their name. Relax and wait. You may or may not hear their answer immediately. If you don't hear it after ten minutes, try again, this time requesting they share it with you loudly and clearly, making it easier for you to clairaudiently hear. Keep trying until you hear something. It might just be a sound and not a name or possibly a whisper that's not as pronounced as you would have liked. That's okay; just continue to be open to their name.

The fifth day holds special meaning because you are going to get a message. Tune in to your guides, again, and ask them to send you a message. This communication can be guidance of some kind, an answer to a question you may have, or can merely be an acknowledgment of their presence. Continue for at least half an hour to hear what they may have to share with you. Be sure to write down anything your guides have told you so you will remember it afterward.

For the rest of the week, practice all of your clairaudient exercises. You may find that not only have you become more sensitive with your clairaudience, but you've also strengthened your physical hearing.

Manifesting

"I listen to the guidance I receive from the universe!"

. . . .

Clairsentience: How does it feel

One of the most commonly utilized intuitive abilities is clairsentience. This gut-instinct, empathic sense comes in handy when trying to decide on a direction to proceed—literally or a life direction. When we meet someone, we also tap into this psychic perception. Learning to recognize the feeling will help you understand the message you are receiving.

"I'm getting a yucky feeling," I told my client Elizabeth. "I don't think it would make you happy," I continued.

"Well, the only way we could swing buying this new house would be to do it together with my mother-in-law. It's got to work out," Elizabeth replied. "Right now we can't afford it on our own, and this seems to be a great alternative. And I truly feel like we'll be all right. After all, we would be getting a two-family, not a single-family, home."

"Okay, but I have to tell you it doesn't feel right to me. I'm not sure why. Having said that, though, I see you interested in an older home, one that needs a lot of work. That's where your heart is. But I feel you will get a newer, ranch-style or cape-style house. Blue or grayish," I told her, knowing for some reason the situation would not last.

They bought the house together, and it worked well for a while, until years later when the house was lost to the bank, as so many others have been, due to the rapid downturn in the economy. It wasn't so much that I saw it being a terrible idea to purchase the home together; it was more that I felt it would turn "icky," and unfortunately it did.

The good thing that came out of the time we spent together was that Elizabeth began a career in a field in which she is truly able to inspire others to reach their potential and help thousands of people to come together for a very worthy and important cause—cancer research. Everything happens for a reason, and I believe this was a big part of her need to experience what she did, unbeknownst to her (or me) at the time.

That yucky or icky feeling is what I get when I don't think something will work out. Not because I feel it's terrible or that it can't work, but because I feel it's not for the best. I also experience this sensation during many relationship questions. Often I'll have people ask me about a new boyfriend or girlfriend and whether it will last. If I get that yucky feeling, I know my clairsentience is telling me they will not be good together. Alternatively, if I experience a warm, fuzzy feeling, I know the relationship has great potential!

I experience clairsentience and am able to associate the feelings I have with this sixth sense easily because I tap into it on a regular basis due to my client sessions. You may not tune in as much and may be more apt to ignore or not recognize these feelings as intuitive senses. But they are. And the more you access your clairsentience, the more prevalent it will become.

When manifesting, or bringing something into your life that you want, using your psychic feeling becomes important. It's helpful to understand if what you are asking for will be good for you or worth your time. Tuning in to your clairsentient abilities can create access to that knowledge.

• •

WEEK 16 EXERCISE:

WHICH PSYCHIC SENSE DO I USE?—CLAIRSENTIENCE

As always, get comfortable and perform your protection meditation. Get out those crayons again. As you hold each shade, looking at the color, see how it makes you feel. Does it feel warm? Cool? Happy? Sad? Angry? Excited? Sick? Energized? A combination? Once you've established how each of the six shades makes you feel, mix them up and close your eyes. One by one, hold a crayon in your hand and focus on how you feel. How does your body feel? How does your hand feel? By using your clairsentience to tune in, see if you can intuit which crayon you have. Continue trying and, as before, if you aren't getting anything psychically, imagine you are! Remember: opening up your mind allows you to be freer when it comes to your intuition.

On the second day, you're going to tap into your clairsentience by using temperature. Get pictures together of various climates that are hot, warm, cold, freezing, wet, dry, humid, arid, and so on. If you don't have pictures, draw some. Be sure not to include any words, as you don't want to use your clairaudience. Now, pick up the shuffled pictures, one by one, and explore how you feel, clairsentiently. See if you experience any temperature or psychic environmental changes. After you've gone through all of the pictures, do it again, and again, and again, until you're comfortable with how you did.

For the next day's exercise, get a friend to join you. Sit down with them, and give them a few moments to conjure up a memory from their life in which there was a high level of emotion. Tell them to try and recall how they felt without saying anything aloud. Now it's your turn to intuit the emotion they are experiencing. Try and feel how they feel, whether it's happiness, sadness, anger, wistfulness, excitement, fear, or another emotion. Repeat this with your friend's additional experiences. Also take a turn at recalling your own memories. Sometimes, in order to understand how someone else feels, we have to be able to relate it to an emotion we've had.

For the rest of the week, repeat the exercises, keeping a written record over the next few days of how you were able to tune in. At the end of the week, note which emotion as well as which exercise felt the cleanest, the clearest, or the most prevalent. Be sure to follow up by clearing whatever empathies or empathic emotions have clung to your energy by invoking, yet again, the white light of protection.

Manifesting

"I am excited because I feel _____

in my future."

(Fill in the blank with your vision of your personal future
as it applies to your greatness!)

✍

• •

Claircognizance: I know

Similar to clairsentience is *claircognizance*, or clear knowing. Everyone has it; it may just need a bit of refining for you to be able to use it. It's that sense of just knowing something even though you have no idea how you know it.

My client Stacey came in for a private reading. Before every session, I take a couple of minutes to tune in to a client's energy psychically and write down information that comes to me, using my intuitive senses. The first thing I wrote down for Stacey was "Divorced." Then I crossed that out, because I worried if she wasn't divorced, it might have caused her to become worried there was something wrong with her marriage. After all, I didn't have any other thoughts or clairvoyant or clairaudient confirmation that what I wrote was right.

When she sat down, I gave her my spiel about how I conduct my readings and what to expect from me. I explained how I write things down before clients walk in, and that usually the information I gleaned during that time will crank open up the energy during the session and help to answer any possible questions. I asked if that worked for her.

She replied, "Great, I'm excited!"

To which, of course, I blurted, "You're divorced!" and then my hand went up to my mouth to catch the foot that had just inserted itself.

"Wow … well, yes I am!" she responded, and it looked like a weight fell from her shoulders.

When I initially tuned in to her energy I wrote "Divorced" because I just knew it. There were no other psychic clues. I didn't see anything, hear anything, or feel anything. I just knew, without a doubt, that she was divorced. That is, until I started questioning myself.

Claircognizance is one of the most challenging senses to believe, because there is really no other validation that what you are receiving is correct. When Stacey sat down, she was ready and open for whatever I channeled for her. Because of this, I couldn't help but blurt out what I knew to be true. Luckily, I trusted in my psychic senses and let my claircognizance do the work. The reading went very well after that!

Simply knowing something can assist you in creating your life. Knowing allows us to feel "right" even if something feels "wrong." Sometimes we want to manifest things that may not be in alignment with our spiritual journey. The ability to know whether we are on the right path can help us determine exactly what we need to build for ourselves. Identifying your natural intuitive slant will be easier once you've practiced using all of your psychic senses. Sometimes we don't know what we've got until it shows itself. Intuition is like this.

- -

WEEK 17 EXERCISE:

WHICH PSYCHIC SENSE DO I USE?—CLAIRCOGNIZANCE

It's time to practice your claircognizance. On the first night of the week, empty your mind, and grab a crayon. What is the first thought, image, sound, or feeling you get? This is the knowing. Don't discount the first message you get. Just know. This may feel difficult or even weird at first, but continue letting it flow. Again, don't worry; doubt is normal. But be sure to be kind to yourself; this is practice.

For the next four nights, tune in to a friend's energy. Tell them whatever you receive claircognizantly. For example, if all of a sudden you think of baseball, ask them what baseball means to them. There's usually no rhyme or reason to what you'll get when you're tuning in with your claircognizance. Just let it flow.

On the sixth night, practice using all of your psychic senses together by closing your eyes, picking up a crayon, and intuiting which color you are holding. Do this at least twenty times and keep track of how many you get correct and how you received the information. Determine whether you used your clairvoyance, clairaudience, clairsentience, or claircognizance. You may find that there are one or two senses that tend to come more naturally.

On the last night of the week, focus on the psychic sense that seems most prevalent to you. Practice using that intuitive sense with a friend by having them pick the crayons for you. You may find that it's easier to tap into your natural abilities with someone else's energy pitching in.

Manifesting

"I know my greatness is within me.
I am confident my greatness is within me.
I know the universe is manifesting my greatness right now."

✍

Chapter 4

Using Intuition

(WEEKS 18–21)

Using Your Intuition

There really is only one simple way to begin tuning in to your intuitive awareness; start using it! It's as simple as that. We know that intuition is real. You've proved it to yourself, I hope, over and over again. What you need to do now is understand how you utilize these psychic senses every day.

Use it for goodness' sake

I was walking with my friend Tracy the other day. We were talking about my first book, *The Book of Psychic Symbols: Interpreting Intuitive Messages*, and how she was really enjoying it, especially the exercises. She then went on to tell me about her own psychic experience.

"I was downstairs doing the laundry, and all of a sudden I got a chill. There were goose bumps all over my body," she said.

"Wow! Was there someone there with you?" I asked her.

"I'm not sure, but it was kind of weird! I knew all of a sudden that I had to go up and call my aunt," she continued.

"Well, that's interesting. I hope you did," I replied.

"I did. I called her, and the second she picked up, I asked her who was pregnant or who was getting married! She was like, 'Oh my God! How did you know your cousin was pregnant? She's only five weeks! We weren't going to tell anyone yet!'"

"That's cool! So, were you excited?"

She answered with disbelief, "I'm just not sure what it's all about. I don't know why I felt that or why I had to call her."

Intangibles

Tracy is not the first one to question why these psychic flashes occur, and she definitely won't be the last. Questioning where it's coming from or how it happens is logical. It's that part of our brain that likes to tie things up neatly, in a package we can hold. That makes it all tangible. It's the intangibles that we have the problem with.

Even though Tracy's psychic feelings were confirmed, she still wondered why it happened. Our intuitive senses are always there; it's just that some people are more aware of them. Often, the biggest psychic hit we'll get is not something huge; it's usually more of a gentle nudge.

Those little ideas, thoughts, or feelings we have can increase our happiness in life—that is, when we listen to them. For instance, imagine that you are at the supermarket and walk past the milk, thinking to yourself, "Hmmm. I wonder if I should get some," but you talk yourself out of it. "No, we had a half-gallon still at home." But when you get home, you see that the kids and all their friends used the milk in their cereal and it's all gone. You realize that now you'll have to drink your coffee black. And anyone who is not a coffee drinker because they love the flavor will understand that black coffee tastes a whole lot different than coffee with milk or cream! You should have listened to your intuition.

The desire to live a more fulfilling life is often what attracts people to living their authentic intuitive selves. This also leads to manifesting not only short-term abundant windfalls but also long-term, life-altering greatness. In the previous story about the pregnant cousin, Tracy didn't really gain anything tangible by listening to messages, but she attained wisdom and insight into a different reality beyond what she may have been used to. She now has a belief that there is more out there, in the ether, and that we are able to grasp and take what we need or want from the universe to help us. It is with great comfort that we are able to comprehend the vastness of our reach.

Using your intuition should not be a limiting practice; you can utilize this knowing sense for more than random flashes or insignificant information. When you become familiar with what your intuition feels like, what it can bring you, you will be better able to control it. Once you've understood this, the world is yours!

• •

WEEK 18 EXERCISE:

USE YOUR INTUITION TO INCREASE YOUR ABUNDANCE

For the next week, you are going to use your intuition to tune in to abundance. In simple terms, you will let your intuition guide your decisions and choices of what you should be focused on, what you should increase, what you should decrease, what you should aim for, and what you should let go of.

Each day, or evening, sit down, and start by bringing your protective bubble around you, warming you and keeping you safe from any negativity. Then, and this may be difficult at first, sit with yourself, no distractions. Open up to your intuition by asking the universe to send you thoughts, feelings, images, words, or ideas.

For the first day, ask the universe to help you become aware of where your focus should be for the day. Should you be focused on material aspects of your life such as finances? Career? Or relationship? Family? Or deeper? Spirituality? Health?

Let your psychic senses tune in to what is most prevalent for you now. Once you have a clear image, thought, or feeling about what it is your gut is telling you, start asking the questions. In order to better that aspect of your life, what should you increase, decrease, aim for, and let go of? Finally, ask the universe to help you intuitively understand what you can focus on symbolically to help with all of those tasks. For example, if you are working on creating a greater connection with family, what image, thought, or feeling can you focus your attention on that will help you accomplish that? Maybe it's an image, like a photograph of a happy family, or maybe it's an abstract art statue of many people holding hands in a circle. Possibly, it's as simple as a yellow smiley face. Whatever the symbol is, continue to pour all of your focus into it throughout the day or evening. This brings your awareness back to your intention and helps strengthen it.

Continue this practice for the week, allowing your intuition to choose a different subject or personal matter six of the seven days. Write down what you focused on throughout the week. On the last day, go over everything you've accomplished! You may find that there were similarities connecting each day or that every meditation provided different themes. Either way, what felt right to you? What felt the best? Also, did anything feel wrong, or upset your intuitive or even physical balance? Do you feel better equipped to deal with your own existence? No matter the outcome, know that you are evolving. You are headed in a direction where intuition meets manifestation, and there will be no option other than greatness!

Manifesting

"I love that I'm an intuitive being."

. . . .

Practicing with Results

We need to choose our own reality. We can opt to follow our rational or logical senses, which quite often are fear-based, and disregard that sometimes nagging voice that directs us to take a different path. Or we can decide to allow intuition to influence our way of life and take the journey that, though not always the easy one, feels most right. The reality is intuition is the thing that tells you that you have come into your own power. It's the incredible spark you feel when you're doing something that's on, rather than something that's off. Intuition guides us, gently or forcefully, to the route we need to be on to fulfill our needs, all the while directing us toward our personal greatness.

Intuition often contradicts what we believe to be our logical sense. But, for most people, not following your gut instincts toward success can create more of a task than paying attention to it. When we go against our natural intuitive senses, we generate speed bumps along the way. This makes it even harder to proceed and get back in line with our spiritual directives. Alternatively, using your intuition allows an organic flow to occur, freeing us from stressors that arise when we fight that course. This, then, becomes the logical route.

Just do it

Tricia, a world-renowned author and speaker as well as my client, called me one day to validate her intuition. She had originally been scheduled to fly from the East Coast to California to be a keynote speaker at a large conference. The producers of the conference had since downgraded her to be a regular presenter in order to allow someone else the opportunity, as Tricia had done it two years in a row. As this was something she was not getting paid for but would instead cost her thousands, she politely declined.

Months later, synchronicities surrounding the conference began to pop up. A colleague, who lived close to the conference location and was on her deathbed, contacted Tricia to let her know she was hoping to see her. Tricia was also asked to speak at another engagement near the original convention, which presented an opportunity to sell her books as well. She had previously decided she was no longer going to book gigs where she wasn't making significant money to cover her expenses and her lost clients while away from her office, and where she was not a keynote, or even a key, speaker. Now, more than ever, she began to second-guess her original decision to bow out of the conference.

Now her intuition was telling her to go, and she needed validation. She contacted me, and I immediately confirmed she needed to "go and don't look back!" This was going to be an incredible opportunity for her, and it would change her life forever in a positive way. She agreed, but needed that extra push. She went online and booked airline tickets, which normally would have been around $800 round trip but were only $240. Everything was falling into place.

Immediately following that, she called the producers of the original conference and asked them if she could still present. They responded right away and said, "We just had someone else back out due to family issues, and we would love for you to be one of the key speakers. We'd hate to lose you twice!"

Well, Tricia went. She presented at both conventions, was extremely well received, and made valuable connections. She had drinks with television representatives and radio people, as well as facilitators who wished to promote her books and her career on the West Coast.

All in all, she had a very successful trip. Going against her analytical brain and instead listening to her intuition helped her attain these successes and brought her that much closer to realizing her personal success goals. For her, intuition and the manifestation of greatness go hand in hand.

Intuitive alignment

For my family and me, intuitive manifestation plays a key role in our lives as well. After we bought our new home, having seen the location and design intuitively before we found it, I saw yet another home, with my psychic eye, that resembled my grandparents' house. I told my husband, and I described it, including the fact that it had a separate cottage on the property. I told him we would have it and that we would rent out the cottage to a family member to help them out. Logically, we both decided that was not to be, as we had just purchased the house we lived in, but still I had a nagging feeling.

Within three months, we were out on our boat on a lake and I saw a "For Sale" sign on one of the houses, and decided to call the realtor whose name was on the sign. Coincidentally, the house had a detached cottage that was not visible from the water. The realtor, Bob Ward, who, along with his wife, has become more than a realtor to us, then told us he had just listed another house, also with a second home included, and asked if we wanted to see it. We said yes and pulled up to it. It was just like my grandparents' house. We bought it right away. The events were foreseen, but totally unexpected. There was no reason to have even looked if I hadn't received the information intuitively. We manifested the perfect property.

Intuition and manifestation complement each other. It's simply about allowing what feels right to your sixth sense to play a part in the creation of your life. We have a destiny or a path to follow. Allowing our psychic sense to guide us along is what we're supposed to do. When everything is aligned within our spirit, we will be at an optimum place to manifest greatness.

• •

WEEK 19 EXERCISE: PRACTICE CONNECTING
INTUITION WITH MANIFESTATION

It's time to use your intuition to help you manifest something you want. This week you will change your life. Focus on a current problem, one where you have a choice to make. Now, pay attention to how you feel about it. You may notice your gut tells you to choose a certain direction though your brain is interrupting it. It can be something that, despite the fact that you believe it's the logical course to take, just feels wrong to you deep down. This time, instead of letting rationalization rule, you will let your psychic sense guide you. Write down each choice on separate pieces of paper.

The next day, go somewhere quiet and comfortable and surround yourself with protective energy as before. Pick up your first choice, or your logical brain choice. Now, read it out loud three times and close your eyes. Pay attention to how it makes you feel, really feel, deep down inside. Sit with this feeling, repeating in your mind the choice you have written down for at least ten minutes, preferably half an hour to an hour. Record in your journal or paper how it made you feel.

On the third day, repeat the process, but with your gut feeling choice. Notice how it feels inside your body and spirit to let this direction flow through you. Again, sit with it as long as possible, and then record all of the feelings you experienced.

On the fourth day, you may have written down another choice. If this is true, go through the steps again. If not, move on to the next day.

On the fifth and sixth days (possibly the fourth as well) focus in on your different options, one at a time. This time, you will make a decisive vote as to which one feels better. You've probably already begun this process, intuitively, but this step will enhance your resolution. Take the time to write it down, and read it back out loud three times.

On the final day of the week, sit, again, with the circle of protection and focus in your mind on the written decision. Then, imagine the other alternative(s) as they appear on the paper(s) beginning to evaporate, as though they were recorded with invisible ink. Keep visualizing with your intuition that the only choice left is the one that felt the best to you, in every way.

Finally, say the preference out loud again, firming up your resolve to have the situation in your life achieve this outcome. Say it audibly at least ten times in a row, all the while imagining the words getting brighter and bigger, your decision reaching out into the universe.

Manifesting

**"I am exactly where I need to be
on my journey toward greatness."**

. . . .

Fine-Tuning Your Intuitive Awareness

Intuition is void of fear and, strangely enough, hope. This means that intuition is pure, without concern or worry about the outcome. That's how you'll know that you are experiencing true intuition. Yes, you may have the tingling sensation or an out-of-body feeling, but these are the effects of the episode. Intuition in its most basic form is uncontaminated.

Recognizing the sixth sense

All of us experience intuition in one way or another, even if we attribute it to something other than a psychic sense. We may chalk it up to a mother's knowing, or a coincidence, or a hunch or gut instinct. But it's there, always in one form or another. Carl Llewellyn Weschcke and Joe H. Slate, PhD, explained how intuition even plays a part in crime investigation in their book *The Llewellyn Complete Book of Psychic Empowerment*: "Interestingly, such evidence when experienced by investigative psychics is usually attributed to ESP, but when experienced by crime investigators it is often explained as a 'lucky hunch' or simply 'intuition.'" Whether it's deemed to be psychic impressions or intuition or even just a lucky hunch, it's all the same. The information is attained from somewhere.

Intuitive awareness means you recognize how your body and mind feel when you are tuning in to your sixth sense. It means you are conscious of the fact that there is more occurring than rational thought or knowledge can explain. Fine-tuning this awareness allows you to utilize this gift more often, and more precisely, than ever before. By tweaking this sense you will become stronger with all of your senses and more empowered, leading you to a fuller and more expansive sense of purpose.

We don't always acknowledge the guidance we receive because, often, tapping into our intuition can create more questions than clarity. This occurs because it's hard to recognize what our intuition is trying to communicate to us. Sometimes, because of this, people stop trying to tune in. We need to continue accessing this information, though, because it's so important; it permeates throughout our entire existence. Often, we discount our intuitive messages because we believe them to be only our imagination. Penney Pierce shares that intuition comes in all forms, for all aspects of our lives, in her book *The Intuitive Way: the Definitive Guide to Increasing Your Awareness*: "Intuition can as easily bring us highly specific, mundane answers, for example, whom to trust or what not to eat, or an instant understanding of complex intellectual patterns."

Settle down, it'll all be clear

We receive psychic information from our spirit guides, deceased loved ones, angels, God, the universe, and all the ascended masters. They send us messages with the intent that we will comprehend them. Your messengers will often send communications symbolically, using whatever images, thoughts, feelings, sounds, and emotions they're able to use, and they will attempt to correspond by sharing something you can relate to. Understanding the symbolic messages helps to clarify what your psychic sense is picking up.

These messages, more often than not, can be extremely difficult to comprehend. After all, imagine trying to tune in to a radio station from a faraway state; it would be filled with static if it came in at all. Now, imagine that radio station is from a whole different plane of existence. Essentially that's what we're dealing with. Our helpers from the other side want to make it as easy as possible for us, so they will present the messages to us in a way in which we can interpret using our own frame of reference.

Think of symbols like logos. Marketing companies spend a lot of time and money to create symbols for products that will be easily recognized. That's sort of what our guides from the other side do to aid our comprehension of psychic symbols. For example, if you were fascinated with animals but oblivious to automobiles and were trying to visualize an answer to what type of car you should buy that would make you happy, your guides may send you an image of a horse to help you understand Ford Mustang, or a beetle for, of course, a Volkswagen Bug. Imagine how difficult it would be, especially for someone who's not well versed in psychic phenomena, to try and understand "Volkswagen." An image of the bug is much simpler.

I often teach a workshop called "Playing with Psychic Symbols." During a recent class I had a student ask me what I picked up on for her. I told her I was seeing water flowing and converging around her, causing disruption. I also told her I believed this was in both her physical and her mental life.

"Does this make sense to you?" I asked this student, Patty.

"Well, it's very interesting because there was just flooding everywhere around our town due to the recent storms," she replied, but then continued, "and I have this dream where I'm driving along on the road and all of a sudden water comes flooding in from both sides and I can't see the road anymore, but I feel like I have to keep going and fight my way through even though it's really hard."

Now, to me, this makes perfect sense. Water is about emotion, and having the water come and block her path was very significant, so I continued with my explanation.

"You are on a journey, but it's difficult to know what's coming up for you and that makes you crazy! Everything feels like a struggle. Water indicates emotion, and there are many emotional blocks right now. Just loosen up, sit back, and enjoy the ride. Sometimes you are not meant to control and steer, but instead are meant to just go with the flow. The effort will be lessened that way."

"I hate letting go!" she pleaded, as if I could help her retain the control in some way.

"Well, it's entirely your choice. You can struggle and try and continue without seeing where you're going, or you can relax and take advantage of not having to worry, knowing that the universe is providing your direction! Enjoy the freedom!" I laughed.

"Ugh. Fine, but that universe better know what it's doing!" Patty replied, giving in and knowing full well there was no other option for her anyway.

The messages I received for her were intuitive in that I psychically saw the flooding and I was also tuning in to her symbolic imagery, through my own clairvoyant visions and her dreams. The images were both physical and emotional in nature, and allowed me to understand and interpret them in multiple ways that held great meaning for Patty.

Intuition is not some esoteric idea that has no basis in reality. In truth, you must be grounded in reality to access your abilities. Developing a relationship with your psychic awareness can mean the difference between coming up against roadblocks or happily sailing through life. Examining the meaning behind the symbols will give you the key to unlocking your own personal sixth sense and may be a pivotal turning point to the potential possibilities that fine-tuning your intuition can provide.

• •

WEEK 20 EXERCISE:

FINE-TUNING YOUR INTUITION

It's time to evolve! On the first day of this week, get outside. Fine-tuning your intuition is not just about sitting in a meditative state and trying to connect; it's about being part of nature. Go for a solitary walk, preferably in the woods. It doesn't matter what type of weather, just be outside. As you walk, make each step count. With each placement of your right foot, exhale, and with your left foot, inhale. Do this for at least ten minutes. Let your pace match your breath. You may notice you are having thoughts or feelings as you walk. Just let them come. Don't try and work at it. Just focus on your breath and your path.

On the second day, go outside again! This time as you walk, think of a question to which you really want an answer. After you've designed your question so as to have an answer other than "yes" or "no," begin focusing on the words *clarity* and *vision* with every step.

Decide on your question as you walk, and then focus, alternatively with your right foot on the word *clarity* and with your left foot the word *vision*. As you do, you are opening yourself up to receiving symbolic response. Continue alternating between asking your question and then saying the words *clarity* and *vision*. Don't try and come up with an answer yet. You are stating your question to the universe—give it time to sink in.

On the third day, you are going to fine-tune that awareness. Sit, and be still, outside or in—but, above all, be comfortable. Think about your question and the possible or probable answers to that question. Now, allow yourself to experience how the different answers make you feel. Sit until you feel how *all* of the possible answers affect you. Do they make you feel good? Bad? Do you see what each answer can bring exponentially, as the effect ripples outward? Sit with your thoughts, consciously breathing in and out until you fully comprehend the potentiality of the different directions.

On the fourth day, walk again. Remember, this can be anywhere: in the woods, on the city streets, in the gym, or on the local high school track, but do it alone. Now, in your mind, tell yourself you want to receive intuitive guidance, preferably symbolic so that you can easily comprehend the messages you'll be given. Your messages may be coming from your higher self, the universe, or even your various guides and deceased loved ones. Set your intention that you want to be shown truthful and helpful symbolic answers. You may see an image, feel a sensation, hear a sound or a word or a song, or even smell something. Walk until you become intuitively aware that there is an answer floating around you waiting to be understood.

During the rest of the week, write down every symbolic thought, feeling, image, and so forth that you experienced, and review them. Did the symbols make sense? Did you understand them? Do you need to sit or walk again to receive additional guidance?

Do the answers you were given resonate with you? Do you feel they clarified your situation? Do they help you? It's not always going to be the answer you are looking for, but it will help you learn to distinguish your hopes from your true intuition. Don't forget: intuition doesn't assimilate hopes and fears. It merely is. It answers with a universal truth that doesn't take into account what you want to happen so much as it provides you with what will happen and what can happen based on your decisions and choices. It is up to you whether to follow it!

Manifesting

"I am open to all the messages from the universe."

Believing in Possibilities: Intuition, Signs, and Synchronicity

It is truly up to you to believe in the possibilities that intuition is real, and that opening to your intuition can bring you great solace and joy. Whether you choose to call it by its name *intuition* or not isn't an issue. It's still intuition, that sixth sense, and taking the opportunity to breathe it in will advance your life and your life's purpose.

When the airplane was first invented, no one believed it would fly, but it did. Luckily, believing in your intuition is not as difficult! Following through and changing your life is the next logical step. Sharon Klingler states it simply in her book *Intuition and Beyond: A Step-by-Step Approach to Discovering Your Inner Voice*: "The action of trust begins with believing—or at least seriously considering—your intuitive perceptions. But belief is only the beginning. You must then act on that trust; you must respond!"

You have the power

Now that you are acutely aware that there is more to this life than meets the physical senses, it's time to act on this awareness. You have the power to create, and the power to interpret. You can choose your destiny and make it one that works for you. The possibilities are endless! You're born with only your physical body and your senses. It is your choice to create what your life will be. There is no reason as you grow up that this has to change.

Fear has a way of blocking us from recognizing and interpreting our intuition and the signs that are sent to us. It also hinders progress when manifesting. Believing that we can have something or reach a goal or achieve our dreams or desires is critical to manifesting what we want. If we are fearful that it won't happen or we don't deserve it or even that the process won't work in order to bring about what we want, then chances are we won't get it. Losing the fear and coming instead from a place of believing and, by extension, love will produce better manifestation results 100 percent of the time. Fear is a strong deterrent; you need to make believing in the possibilities stronger.

Believing in something means you have to have faith that it is real, that whatever you believe in has merit. Arguably, accepting synchronicities as more than coincidence requires a faith that there is something, some universal force, working behind the scenes to create these concurrent events.

A man recently wrote to me with questions regarding a series of synchronistic events he had experienced. He had called the police department at his house two nights in a row—the first night a false alarm, the second for a real issue. Thankfully, it was small, an attempted auto break-in by local teenagers who were immediately remorseful and apologetic. Next, he went to a wake because a co-worker's wife had died, and it turned out she was a retired policewoman and the funeral home was filled with other officers. A couple of days later he went to a fundraiser, and the man who invited him, just an acquaintance from the gym, along with his wife, were also police officers. He finally wrote to me because he received an email that another co-worker's husband had died. He went to the wake and funeral and, lo and behold, the deceased was another retired officer! Then, to top it all off, immediately before I read his email, I had been talking with my husband about a food booth at a local festival. Every year this particular booth has the best baked potatoes, and it is sponsored by the local police station. Synchronistic events are there for a reason. Taking notice of them means you believe there's more to them then simply coincidence.

Signs are also important. They are the little or sometimes big things you notice when pondering a question or direction.

One of the best signs I ever had appeared when I was deciding whether to take a gig in New York City or not. Financially, it wasn't beneficial, at least in the short term, but I thought it would be a great opportunity. I just didn't know if I wanted to commit. As I was driving along, I thought to myself, "I need a sign, something that will help me decide if I should take this leap." Almost immediately, I came upon a billboard that, no lie, said, *If you are looking for a sign, this is it!* Needless to say, I did the appearance and it was very well received.

Considering synchronicities and signs as gentle nudges from the universe affords us the opportunity to prove intuition as well. It's kind of a circular process: a synchronistic event is recognized, which connects us to our intuition, which then allows us to witness and acknowledge synchronicities, and so on and so on.

Sign of the times

I'm usually in bed between 11 p.m. and midnight, and I normally read for a while. A recent night was different. I went to bed around 10 p.m. and tried to read, but my book kept falling on my face because sleep was calling. I was snoozing by 10:15. Jumping up, out of my sound sleep, I swore I heard a noise. I looked around and noticed the time on my clock: 11:11. Now, what makes this even more interesting is that it was November 11. So, 11/11, 11:11. Twitter had been blowing up all day about making a wish at 11:11 on 11/11, so I quickly nudged my husband and said, "Make a wish!" He immediately, though half-asleep, knew what I was talking about, and together, yet separately, we made our wishes.

Before I went to bed, I had tried to tune in for my husband to see if he was going to get a check that week for a custom cabinetry job he was starting. I couldn't really understand the answer. After wishing at 11:11 on 11/11, I knew, without hesitation, that he was going to be getting a check in the mail, and soon. We both wished for this to happen, and that next morning, upon waking, he got a text saying the check was going out! This was a sign, a sign that everything was going to be good. It also helped with the manifestation of money. It opened my intuition to let me access the answers.

Sometimes, receiving a sign helps us to tune in to our intuition. Signs are different from symbols, though both are communications to aid us in knowing if we are on the right track or to help guide us toward success. Symbols are messages we psychically perceive internally with our sixth sense, whereas signs are messages we physically perceive externally with our eyes or ears.

Synchronicities around the world

Alli lives in South Africa. She had picked up a copy of my book *The Book of Psychic Symbols: Interpreting Intuitive Messages* and immediately began experiencing synchronistic events before she even opened to page 1. She took it as a sign that she needed to buy it right then and there, though she had heard of it already and normally would have purchased and downloaded it on her Kindle. Buying the book brought back the memory of an intuitive reader she had visited many years previously in South Africa, and she began wishing she could have another session with her. Soon afterward, she received a random text message from that very same psychic that she would be in Johannesburg, in a different part of the country, on December 1.

As chance, though never random, would have it, Alli was celebrating an early Christmas with her company the day before in Johannesburg and was scheduled to fly back home the evening of December 1. She was able to book her reading.

During the first chapter and first exercises, she wrote down how she felt about intuition: "Mixed feelings. I believe in it, but frequently ignore it only to realize later what I had done. I over-think and make it about logic and give myself options based on fact instead of going with my intuition … And my lesson today? Stop overanalyzing, recognize your gift and work with it!" As Alli said, it's time to just accept intuition and embrace it as part of everyday life. It can be logical, as long as we allow it to be. She realized, too, that by opening herself to her intuition, she was able to manifest something she really wanted.

Through a series of serendipitous events, Alli was able to experience signs, synchronicity, manifestation, and intuition. She learned or, more accurately, re-learned that they go hand in hand. Believing these gifts were possible, even with a touch of skepticism, allowed her to have unique opportunities that tuned her in to her sixth sense.

. . . .

WEEK 21 EXERCISE: RECOGNIZING INTUITION, SYNCHRONICITIES, AND SIGNS TO MANIFEST

Putting it all into action is what this next week is all about. You know all about signs, synchronicities, and intuition, so let's practice recognizing them to help manifest.

On the first day, ask a question aloud that you want answered. Make it about a real issue, something of importance to you. Then, write it down; writing it down helps to put it out into the universe. Now, focus on the question and everything it entails. This is not about tuning in to your psychic awareness or looking for signs; it is merely about exploring your question in your mind.

On the second day, it's time to find answers to that question. Begin looking for signs that will point you toward some kind of response. They may be as grand as a billboard or as small as a butterfly. Whatever the signs are, they will hold meaning, not only generalized but also specific meaning for you, personally. Continue throughout the day, looking for those signs. Don't, however, make them up. They will be there. Write them down on a fresh page, after your question.

On the third day, explore for synchronicities. You may begin to notice, or may have already experienced, synchronistic events regarding this question. For example, if you are asking if you should pursue a relationship with someone, and as you're talking with that person your ex with whom you had a bad relationship shows up, you might list that as a negative synchronicity. Alternatively, if you are talking about the current flame and all of a sudden a priest walks into the room and says, "So, when are you getting married?" that may be a positive synchronistic event. Write them all down.

On the fourth day, make a list. Write down all of the occurrences of signs and synchronicities. Make a list as to how they relate to your question. For example, if you asked a question that requires a yes or no answer, sort your intuitive data into yes or no pages. If your question is about direction, one way or another, configure your lists so the information drops into the correct spot. Be sure to record all of your experiences from the past couple of days.

On the fifth day, it's time to tune in to your intuition to help guide you toward an answer based on all of the data. Before you start, be sure to go somewhere quiet and comfortable. Ground yourself by bringing in your circle of white light. Go down your lists, one at a time, and notice how each experience felt. Whether it was a sign or a synchronicity, write down next to it whether it makes you feel happy, sad, mad, frustrated, excited, and so on. Make sure to take your time with this. It's very important to get a true intuitive feeling.

Now, on the sixth day, it's decision time. You've gone over all of the signs and synchronicities and tuned in to your intuition. By now you should be ready to make a choice that feels right to you. Write the original question down, again, with authority. Then write your answer! Does it feel right? Does it feel the way you expected it to?

On the final day of the week, let's bring it home. It's the perfect chance to practice your basic manifestation skills. You already know what you want, or what your answer is. You are going to work on making your decision a positive reality. Sit in a comfortable position and close your eyes. Visualize in your mind what you've chosen as your answer. Now, imagine the answer you've chosen surrounded by a beautiful pink bubble of energy. Send love to your decision. Watch as that bubble grows, getting sparkly and almost electrically charged. Feel the energy emanating from the bubble as it continues getting bigger and bigger. Create a funnel-like shape, again in your mind, originating from your abdomen, which stretches all the way into the bubble. Imagine a flow of energy, almost like liquid traveling from your funnel into the bubble, extending even further as it goes to create a connection of creative sparks. Send through that funnel love and intention—the intention that your decision or the answer you've received will bring the best possible outcome for you. Continue doing this while now saying aloud the words, "This is for my better good, and will be in my greatest interests. The outcome and effects of this will bring only positivity." Repeat this ten times, more if you're able, and then detach the funnel from your abdomen and watch the incredible large, glowing, pink bubble float away into the universe, carrying your answer, your outcome, to be fulfilled as fact.

Bonus

You have completed an incredible cycle this week and may feel exhausted. Take this evening, and possibly the next day, to relax. Lie down in a comfortable position and shut your eyes. Imagine a beautiful white light traveling and circling around you. Visualize this light stretching beyond where the eye can see, up into the sky, extending all the way to the sun.

Feel, now, the warmth of the sun, shining down on you through this light. As this power of the sun streams through you and around you, feel the warmth that it brings. Allow the sun's rays to rejuvenate and revitalize you. Feel the light as it permeates through every cell of your skin and down into your muscles and bones and even your internal organs. Allow the healing energy of the sun to replace whatever energy you've spent this week and restore you to your rightful state, a powerful, magnificent human being. Whenever you are ready, you can open your eyes, eager to continue, feeling refreshed and vibrant and happy to be you.

Manifesting

"I know everything happens for a reason because

_____."

(Fill in the blank!)

Chapter 5
Strengths and Motivations
(WEEKS 22–27)

Core Values

Identifying core values is extremely important in manifesting greatness. Just like determining what you believe success to be, what we deem necessary values for ourselves plays a key role in being able to achieve anything. Everyone has an unwritten set of core values. It is this set of values that guides us in our lives even if we've never identified them before.

Chaos or clarity

Understanding what's essential assists us in interpreting different events in our lives, and whether we agree or disagree with how they were handled. "Without values there is confusion and chaos. When values disintegrate, everything disintegrates," Deepak Chopra writes in his book *Creating Affluence.* Can you imagine a world where nothing was valued? That world would surely fall apart, as Chopra states.

Our values influence and are the driving force in our life. They dictate how we live and the company we keep. They are the ethics we strive to adhere to. They are the standards by which we set our goals.

Without values we would have no gauge with which to set our goals. In fact, our values direct our goals—what we desire to have.

Pride stems from authenticity and being at one with your beliefs. It also catapults your self-esteem and promotes happiness. I'm not talking about ego, which comes from a totally different place. Ego has more to do with others than with yourself, whereas true pride stems from aligning your path with your core. Being proud of yourself can help you feel confident. It can give you a sense of security and fill you with self-esteem.

We are born with principles. We don't always follow them, but when we do, it just feels right. These central beliefs can change as we get older and experience life. But most of us share a set of ideas that complement each other, such as kindness, family, health, honesty, and friendship. These are the principles for which we adjust our lives to accomplish. Within these basic core values are more defined and streamlined values, but the basics always stay the same. For example, within kindness lies caring for others, supporting a good cause, love, and the like.

For most people, it doesn't have to be "either/or." For instance, if success is not one of your essential core values, it doesn't mean you value failure. It simply means success is not something that's necessary for you to live an authentic life, as you see it. However, success, as we've noted in the earlier chapters, has many connotations and is not always connected to finances. Being successful can represent being happy and content in a relationship. Leave room for translation, before judging what you do or don't have in your set of values, or you may create an ethical conundrum for no reason.

Being the best you that you can be is dependent upon being in alignment with your set of core values. "You can pretend to be something other than which you are, but eventually you will run out of energy to continue because that's not authentically you," as author Caroline Myss puts it. When you're out of balance with your values, your life will feel out of control; nothing will make sense or feel right. But it doesn't have to stay that way.

Setting your life to be congruent with your beliefs can create a positive spin. By tuning in to your set of principles, you will open up immense opportunities to manifest the greatness you so deserve.

• •

WEEK 22 EXERCISE:

IDENTIFYING WHAT'SIMPORTANT TO YOU

Before being able to work with your core values, you have to begin to understand what they are for you, personally. So, on the first day of Week 22, you are going to create a list of your fifty core values. It may seem like a lot, but it's important to be expansive at first so you don't overlook anything that's truly relevant to who you are.

Write down your fifty core values. Be detailed, but don't write them out in sentences. Use only one or two words to describe each. For example, don't write down "Be kind to animals." Instead, just write "animals" as one, and "kindness" as another. They are part of what's important to you. Obviously, if kindness wasn't attached to animals, then animals wouldn't be important to you, unless you were talking about hunting them, in which case "hunting" would be your value.

On the second day, compare your fifty core values to the ones listed below and on the following pages. Do you want to swap some? Go ahead and do that now.

Abundance	Acceptance
Accessibility	Accomplishment
Accuracy	Achievement
Acknowledgment	Activeness
Adaptability	Adoration

Adroitness	Adventure
Affection	Affluence
Aggressiveness	Agility
Alertness	Altruism
Ambition	Amusement
Appreciation	Approachability
Articulateness	Assertiveness
Assurance	Attentiveness
Attractiveness	Audacity
Authenticity	Authority
Autonomy	Availability
Awareness	Awe
Balance	Beauty
Belonging	Benevolence
Bliss	Boldness
Bravery	Brilliance
Buoyancy	Calmness
Camaraderie	Candor
Capability	Care
Carefulness	Certainty
Challenge	Charity
Charm	Chastity
Cheerfulness	Choice
Clarity	Cleanliness
Cleverness	Closeness
Collaboration	Comfort
Commitment	Compassion
Competition	Composure
Confidence	Conformity
Congruency	Connection
Consciousness	Consistency

Contentment	Continuity
Contribution	Control
Conviction	Conviviality
Cooperation	Cordiality
Correctness	Courage
Courtesy	Craftiness
Creativity	Credibility
Cunningness	Curiosity
Daring	Decisiveness
Decorum	Deference
Delight	Dependability
Depth	Desire
Determination	Devotion
Devoutness	Dexterity
Dignity	Diligence
Directness	Discipline
Discretion	Diversity
Dominance	Drive
Duty	Dynamism
Eagerness	Economical
Ecstasy	Education
Effectiveness	Efficiency
Elation	Elegance
Empathy	Encouragement
Endurance	Enjoyment
Entertainment	Enthusiasm
Excellence	Excitement
Exhilaration	Expediency
Expertise	Exploration
Expressiveness	Extravagance
Extroversion	Exuberance

Fairness	Faith
Fame	Family
Fascination	Fearlessness
Ferocity	Fidelity
Fierceness	Financial Success
Firmness	Fitness
Flexibility	Fluency
Focus	Fortitude
Frankness	Freedom
Friendliness	Friendship
Frugality	Fun
Gallantry	Generosity
Gentility	Giving
Grace	Gratitude
Gregariousness	Growth
Guidance	Happiness
Harmony	Health
Heart	Helpfulness
Heroism	Holiness
Honesty	Honor
Hopefulness	Hospitality
Humility	Humor
Hygiene	Imagination
Impartiality	Independence
Industrious	Influence
Ingenuity	Ingenuity
Innovation	Inquisitiveness
Insightfulness	Inspiration
Integrity	Intelligence
Intensity	Intimacy
Introversion	Intuition

Inventiveness	Investing
Joy	Judiciousness
Justice	Keenness
Kindness	Knowledge
Leadership	Learning
Liberation	Liberty
Liveliness	Logic
Longevity	Love
Loyalty	Majesty
Mastery	Maturity
Meekness	Mellowness
Meticulousness	Mindfulness
Modesty	Motivation
Mysteriousness	Nature
Neatness	Nerve
Nurture	Openness
Obedience	Optimism
Order	Organization
Originality	Outlandishness
Outrageousness	Passion
Peace	Perceptiveness
Perfection	Perkiness
Perseverance	Persistence
Persuasiveness	Philanthropy
Piety	Playfulness
Pleasantness	Pleasure
Poise	Popularity
Power	Practicality
Pragmatism	Precision
Preparedness	Presence
Privacy	Proactivity

Productivity	Professionalism
Prosperity	Prudence
Punctuality	Purity
Realism	Reason
Reasonableness	Recognition
Recreation	Refinement
Reflection	Relaxation
Reliability	Religiousness
Resilience	Resolution
Resolve	Resourcefulness
Respect	Restraint
Reverence	Richness
Rigid	Romance
Sacredness	Sacrifice
Sagacity	Saintliness
Sanguinity	Satisfaction
Security	Self-control
Selflessness	Self-reliance
Sensitivity	Sensuality
Serenity	Service
Sexuality	Share
Sharing	Shrewdness
Silence	Silliness
Simplicity	Sincerity
Skillfulness	Solidarity
Solitude	Speed
Spirit	Spirituality
Spontaneity	Spunk
Stability	Status
Stealth	Stillness
Strength	Structure

Success	Support
Supremacy	Surprise
Sympathy	Synergy
Talented	Teamwork
Temperance	Thankfulness
Thoroughness	Thoughtfulness
Thrift	Tidiness
Timeliness	Tolerance
Traditionalism	Tranquility
Transcendence	Trust
Trustworthiness	Truth
Understanding	Unflappability
Uniqueness	Unity
Usefulness	Utility
Valor	Variety
Victory	Vigor
Virtue	Vision
Vitality	Vivacity
Warmth	Watchfulness
Wealth	Willfulness
Willingness	Winning
Wisdom	Wittiness
Wonder	Youthfulness
Zeal	

On the third day, it's time to whittle down that list a bit. Look at your list of fifty and note which items are redundant. For instance, "kindness" and "niceness" would probably be the same thing. Choose which works better for who you are. Streamline that list down to thirty-five. It shouldn't be too difficult, but if it is, really look at it and figure out what is already stated somewhere else.

On the fourth day, it's getting a little tougher. It's time to simplify your list yet again. Using the same methods as above, pare it down to twenty core values. Remember, these are values, not acts. Do not include "Working at a homeless shelter," as this is an *act* of kindness or philanthropy rather than a core value. Instead you may wish to list "compassion" or "charity" as being your value, which may also represent other values you can delete from your list.

Okay, you are ready. Chop your list down even further to ten core values on the fifth day. These should be your most authentic core values. Don't allow this list to be what you "think" it should be, or what you believe others think it should be. This is your list; everyone's is different.

For the rest of the week, notice how these values influence your life and what you do. Write down any actions or events you were involved in that you may have done differently had you not had your values. Think about how you believe the outcome was affected by sticking to your principles. Then, record any significant times you didn't follow your core values. How did it feel? What was the outcome? Were you happy with it?

Manifesting

**"I am karmically in tune with,
and live according to, my values."**

. . . .

My Strengths

More often than not, we enjoy what we're good at. It's far less frequent to enjoy something we are terrible at because it gives us no pleasure to fail or to fail to succeed. This is why it's so important to figure out where your strengths lie without limiting yourself to only what you are fantastic at. This discovery can lead us down a path where receiving gifts from the universe is more abundant.

Your power

Your strengths reside where your power is. Simply stated, you have a power inside of you that gives you strength and allows you to excel. This power, this energy, this force is yours to tweak or utilize as you see fit. Abundance flows into this power center; we just have to recognize it. Rhonda Byrne says in her book *The Power:* "People who have great lives think and talk about what they love *more* than what they don't love!" Focusing on our strengths and what we love creates the space to allow abundance to flow.

Keeping your power reined in can inhibit you from utilizing your strengths to generate what you want. By sharing your gifts with the world, you are expressing who you are. Your actions, and not just your values, represent who you are—not the idea of who you want to be. Bringing these together is key to living a truly abundant life.

You are worthy

When you use your strengths, you get the job done, regardless of what that job is. When you don't use your strengths, the job stops and life comes to a halt. The gears stop turning and begin grinding as everything comes to a standstill. Greatness usually doesn't just magically happen; you need to give it some help by enhancing what you're already good at.

Being a professional skateboarder probably won't happen if you have no sense of balance, but winning awards in photography may if you have an eye for photography. When I do readings for people, I tap into their potential. Potential is based on strengths that are already there, part of who you are.

I did such a reading years ago, with many follow-ups, for a beautiful spirit named Regina. I knew that the job she was leaving was not a good fit for her, but I also knew she would eventually land in a spot that would help her help others, and it would be a type of job where she could help make a difference on a global scale. This was her potential—where she was strong and powerful. Sure enough, though it took many years, she found such a job, or I should say it found her. She is working now to defend the natural resources we take for granted. She is well on her way to manifesting her greatness.

Being a life coach and a hypnotist as well as a professional psychic with a full practice has opened my eyes to how easily we lose our way and begin to doubt our strengths. With each doubting moment, we take a hit to our self-esteem. When we are stuck in a cycle of events or circumstances where we fail instead of succeeding, we can feel our confidence deteriorating. When that happens, it is often difficult to gain the momentum again toward manifesting greatness or even simply enjoying our strength and our power again. We become stagnant in our movements and lose drive. We need to believe we are valuable, and when we don't feel we have strengths to contribute, feeling valuable to society is hard. It helps to have others compliment or recognize what we are good at, or what they appreciate about us, to get us rolling in the right direction.

Barton Goldsmith, PhD, author of *100 Ways to Boost Your Self-Confidence*, shares how appreciating someone else's participation in your own world can increase your feeling of worth: "Helping people feel better about themselves will foster good in every way, shape, and form."

Usually, we won't be attempting to manifest greatness by wishing to create something that's foreign to us. We gravitate, instead, toward what's familiar, though that doesn't mean we have already attained it or we can't go for something that's out of our comfort zone. Simply put, we want to manifest what we're attracted to, and we are attracted to what we enjoy or want for ourselves. When you recognize this, manifesting greatness becomes so much easier.

. . . .

WEEK 23 EXERCISE:

I AM STRONG!

This week will be a little different from the others. This week, for five days, you are going to carry your journal around with you. Whenever the need arises, write down one of your strengths. It's important to give it the full five days because you are a very strong person! You have incredible potential, and it's hard to sum up all of your talent, abilities, and gifts in one day.

Be sure to include all of your strengths and, most importantly, be honest with yourself! If you hit one home run in your life, but rarely do anything else of note when playing ball, don't include that as strength, unless you truly believe it is. After all, there are many supporting roles in ballgames. But if you consistently hit home runs, or get the other team out, or pitch no-hitters, then that can definitely be listed. And don't let anyone else belittle what you believe are your strengths.

On the sixth day, summarize all of the strengths you've listed. Then pick out only those that make you happy and record them. Narrow it down a bit further, and group the strengths together. Using the ballgame example, if you've written that you are really good at baseball, and then you also write you are exemplary at cross-country, you may just want to write "athletic" as one of your strengths.

Finally, after linking and joining your various strengths, look at your journal entry on this last day. What jumps out at you? What feels good? Out of the ones that leap off the page, what can you do with them to pursue greatness? Again, if it's "athletic," does it make sense to chase that in some capacity? What would give you the most joy? This is your potential, what you can create for yourself!

Manifesting

"I am very good at _____."

☺ ✍

. . . .

Better for Everyone

When we strive to become better people, we decide whether it's for us or for somebody else. We derive pleasure from helping others and from bettering other people. Sometimes it's easier for us to do things for others than it is to do things for ourselves. If we have a general slant toward charity work or philanthropy, we may find that helping others is part of virtue calling and something that is in line with our destiny. But there can be a downside; when we do for others from our egocentric place as opposed to our altruistic sense, it becomes more of a benefit-to-cost ratio instead of a truly charitable act. Often it is a mix of both.

Once we determine that we are acting from our true self, we can decide whether or not we need to manifest for the greatness of everybody or whether manifesting greatness is truly an individual act or an individual ideal. Creating, or helping others to create, when you are coming from a selfless place of love and asking for nothing in return is what Einstein referred to when he talked about wanting to think like God thinks. To tune in to your highest self is a gift. Using this gift instead of wasting it will open up many opportunities for you.

Out of the ashes

In December 2012, we experienced a horrific tragedy in our community. In the town next door, an obviously disturbed young man broke into Sandy Hook Elementary School, where he gunned down six adults and twenty first-graders, after having killed his own mother. The energy of this attack was so horrendous, so horrifying, that many people stopped functioning. The holidays were dimmed, and the brave lost children and incredible teachers were prayed for and held in our hearts. Let me just reiterate: there is no way to understand this ghastly tragedy. It was unimaginable.

Yet, out of this unspeakable tragedy, much good was shared. Many people began practicing random acts of kindness. I myself was a recipient of an anonymous gift, and was the giver of gifts as well. People near and far donated their time, their money, their hugs. They sent teddy bears and paper snowflakes to the survivors, and a nearby town quickly renovated and opened a new elementary school so the kids would never have to set foot in the scene of the crime again. Ribbons were made and sold to raise money to help with the fallout and the much-needed therapy for the families, the students, the teachers, and the first-responders who witnessed the aftermath. T-shirts were printed; candles were lit; and specially trained dogs were brought to the memorial for the sole purpose of comforting those present. President Obama flew in and spoke with the families and expressed his honest, heartfelt condolences.

This goodness, this generosity, and the list continues on and on, has opened many eyes to the idea of manifesting good for the benefit of others. Though there is obviously a benefit we receive for helping others, the greater benefit is the feeling we get inside for being just a small helper in creating a new space for the town to continue on, to exist, after they've lost so much.

We learned as a community, and as individuals, to hug our children a bit longer and tighter, to lend a helping hand to our neighbor, and we realize we are alive for an indeterminate amount of time. Especially now, when so many countless people have suffered, it's our turn to give back and try and make life better for everyone. None of this will ever bring back those we've lost, but it will help us move forward.

Manifesting for others seems more possible now. Where a young mother had no extra funds, she has now raised thousands to donate. Determining what we can do to help make life a little easier will in turn help us to make our lives better. There's a feeling deep down inside that can't help but blossom when we do. This feeling, this love that grows inside, assists us in continuing to believe we are worthy and that we do matter—that in the grand scheme of things, every person counts. We can tune in to this love and add to our lives and the lives around us.

One small step

Manifesting greatness is kind of like walking on the moon. As the late astronaut Neil Armstrong said, "One small step for a man, one giant leap for mankind." This should be the mantra for all wishing to help create a better world for themselves and others. Manifesting something for oneself that in turn benefits so many is what we strive for.

It is not selfish to create or have the drive to bring into your life something that will make you happier or more in tune to who you are. It is part of your destiny and your universal right. When it has the added piece of helping others, your providence is expressed that much farther out into the universe, and karmically you will be rewarded with, at the very least, a knowing that you've contributed to the goodness of the world. And the reality is, at its very core, being happy by creating a better life for yourself helps you become a better person. This, in turn, makes everything around you better—and the world, one small step at a time, becomes a better place.

WEEK 24 EXERCISE:

ONE SMALL STEP

This week is all about paying it forward. It's not just about paying it forward for others, but for yourself. On the first day of the week, think about something you really are hoping to manifest or bring into your own life. Now, give it away to someone! Make it a random act of kindness.

For example, if money is something you are interested in bringing in more of, give some away. Around the holidays there are plenty of Salvation Army Santas that have big red buckets along with their bells and will gladly accept your monetary donation. Or make it more personal. Put a $20 bill in an envelope and leave it on someone's windshield with the words, "Manifesting for the better of everyone" written on it. If you can't afford $20, make it $10, $5, or even $1. Just know that by doing this, you are helping someone out. It will come back to you!

On the second day, do it again. This time, however, do something different. If eating healthy is one of your desires on your manifesting list, then pay for the person behind you in line at the local salad bar or at the coffee shop.

On the third day, yup, you guessed it! Do it again! If manifesting a new car is something you want, how about helping the next person out? Pay for the car wash for the person in line behind you, or pre-pay for someone's gas. Even paying for a portion of the gas will elicit a very grateful response from that person!

On the fourth and the fifth days, do it again. You decide what you're going to do, but make sure, as before, that it is a random act of kindness and that it's anonymous. This will allow the receiver to truly appreciate what you are giving them and encourage them to do the same for someone else!

On the sixth day, write it all down. What gifts did you bestow on others? Maybe you dropped a few coins in a homeless person's can or donated your time to help out at a homeless shelter or a soup kitchen. Maybe you made and sold bracelets and donated the proceeds anonymously to a local animal shelter. Maybe you left a manicure gift card on someone's windshield. Maybe you babysat for someone who needed help or you took some kids to the park who otherwise wouldn't have been able to go—even if you didn't feel like it. Maybe, probably, you did something else.

Go back and read over all of your acts of kindness for the past five days. Which one made you feel the best? Which gave you the greatest sensation? Once you've determined that, go ahead and do it again on the final day of the week! Enjoy the love you are spreading. And although you are doing this out of the goodness of your heart, know that you are extending your manifestation out into the world, and chances are you will attract back what you wish to create for yourself as well!

Manifesting

Go out and do good. Every day.
Practice random acts of kindness every day.
Not just for payback or recognition;
do it because it's the right thing to do.

. . . .

Change for Change's Sake

We change our lives because we are ready for something different. Or because we are tired of the way we have been living. Or, still another reason: we no longer like our life in its current state. This is when the need for change is created. Recognizing we need change is step one.

Knowing, and being aware of our current situation, allows us the perfect opportunity for making new and different choices, which in turn provides for change. And if we don't desire or even succumb to the idea of making our life different, we end up stuck. This causes us to be inauthentic; not admitting that change is necessary makes us vulnerable to the inertia of our current situation.

Change, change, change

We are allowed to appreciate where we are now. There is no law that says we can't say, "It's good enough" or "I don't need more than what I currently have." But there is also no reason to not strive for more, and by doing that, change has to occur. You cannot physically, mentally, or spiritually add something and have it not change what was already there.

Most people, myself included, are resistant to change. The reason is simple. Change brings with it a degree of uncertainty. That's why we put it off—instead, we keep the same job; we stay in a loveless marriage; we live in the same house for generations; we keep the same friends. It's easier when we know what to expect. We become comfortable with our current circumstances. Eventually, this comfort can instead begin to feel claustrophobic. Without change, our energy is stagnant. It's stuck, with no outlet.

In order to grow, you need to accept that change is inevitable. Fear has to take a back seat to the opportunity for growth in order to manifest greatness. The reality is that changing for the sake of change is really not the smartest thing to do, but change has to start somewhere. In order to manifest greatness, you have to decide which direction you want to go, which direction could create positive change.

One of the biggest deterrents to creating a new direction or expanding your horizons is believing that doing it "later" will be okay. It's inevitable that later will never come. Putting change off until later really means you are not going to make the leap. Occasionally, starting off slow can be a good compromise. Rarely will you change your entire life instantly, overnight, but you can decide, overnight, to begin the changes.

Just about every question I get during readings has to do with change: "Should I change jobs?" "Will I be better off getting a new job?" "Should I break up with my boyfriend?" "Do I need to move?" "Should I go back to school?" People often know they need to mix up their lives a bit and modify what they're doing, but it's difficult to do this without a glimpse into the future of what the changes will bring and whether it's worth the effort.

Being open to transforming your life can provide you with infinite possibilities. If you are closed to making any adjustments, there can never be greatness. Greatness comes from the expansion of your potential. Merely becoming aware of the magnitude of your potential can create the desire to try to change. This trying can lead to the yearning to manifest and eventually to the greatness that is within you.

"There is no greatness without a passion to be great, whether it's the aspiration of an athlete or an artist, a scientist, a parent, or a businessman," writes Anthony Robbins in his book *Unlimited Power*. You have to decide you want to be the change rather than simply looking toward someone else to create it for you. Being passionate about your own ideas and creativity will set you on the path to change and guide you toward manifesting the greatness you deserve.

• •

WEEK 25 EXERCISE:
FOR GOODNESS' SAKE

You are now just at the halfway point. And at the place where the decision is to stay as you are or use the opportunity to revolutionize your life! On the first day of the week, get your journal ready. Write down everything you don't like about yourself and your life. It can be something as simple as "My fingernails" or a bit more complicated like "My house." Be honest. This is your journal entry; no one else ever has to see it. Make the list from your heart.

On the second day, go over what you wrote the day before. With serious and truthful consideration, cross off anything you wrote that you are not willing to try and change at this time. Know that just because you're crossing it off today doesn't mean you can't revisit it again.

The next day, narrow your list down to only three aspects you are willing to change. Again, be true to yourself. If you feel like you can't commit to adjusting these areas, get rid of them right now; remove them from your page.

You've itemized three things you are prepared to attempt to make different in your life. Today is the day to begin thinking about how you want to adjust each item in your life. Put some thought into your decisions. You are looking toward the end goal, what it is you would like to have instead of what you are hoping to be rid of.

On the fifth, sixth, and seventh days, you will address each item. You don't have to actually manifest the change or go "cold turkey" with what you currently have. Rather, each day, choose one of your three off the list and devise a plan for change. By simply putting together a course of action, you are beginning to hold the space for the adjustments to actually occur. Be proud of yourself! You are taking another step toward creating a great life!

Manifesting

"I am open to change and to changing _____**."**

✍ ☺

Motivating Factors

What motivates you? Motivation is necessary to accomplish most tasks. Most of us are not motivated by the possibility of success alone, or by the desire to create something great. But we are motivated by the desire or the need to change. Sometimes it's intrinsic motivation that helps you get going, and other times it is external motivation. Intrinsic motivation is when there is an internal need or force within that's driving you to do something. Eating, for example, is intrinsically motivated, usually by a physiological need. But what if there are external or even metaphysical factors driving you?

Intuition is a great motivator. It gives us a nudge when we need to alter our course or make something better. Intuition is something we inherently use, though we don't always know that's what we are doing. For instance, when we are lost and we are faced with a fork in the road, how do we know which way to turn? Well, if we are truly lost, and we don't have a real live "tracker" on board, we probably tune in to our gut instincts, or intuition, and turn in the direction we feel pulled. We can even make decisions that can alter the course of our lives based on our intuition.

New believer

I recently had a client come in for a reading. She had read an article about me in the newspaper and decided she wanted to have a psychic session with me. She explained upon arrival that she had no idea why she had come. She'd never done anything like this before, yet she felt a need to book the appointment, so we agreed on a half-hour session.

Usually when I do readings, I will tune in to a client's energy about fifteen minutes ahead of time and write down whatever I pick up psychically about them. I did this for Marah, this client. I also wrote down an initial and a couple versions of a name I was trying to pick up. "L," Lee, Ladona, Loudy. I couldn't quite put my finger on it.

So, there we are in my office, and she's just finished saying she doesn't have any questions and she doesn't have any real belief. "I'm sorry, but I don't think anything will come up!" she says and I begin. I start by telling her how I work and how I will ask her if she has any questions after I've gone over everything I've written down.

"Okay, but it's really all right if you don't get anything because there's really no reason that I had to be here," she replies.

Now, I knew everything had occurred for a reason. In fact, she happened to score an immediate session due to a scheduling adjustment I had to make for another client. This is very unusual. There was definitely more of a motivating factor than either of us was aware of which was working to get her in.

"Well, I felt that you were petite, with brown hair and a ready smile," which she was. "I also got that you have a couple of kids and that you are here even though it caused you a good deal of grief at home. Most of your family doesn't believe in this work, except your mother-in…"

She interrupted me, "Wow! My mother-in-law totally believes in this! My husband, on the other hand, felt it was necessary to cause a huge argument last night that this isn't real; it's a scam. I told him essentially it didn't matter what he thought because I was the one having the reading, paying with my own money, and he had no say in it anyway! It got so heated that we still aren't talking today!"

"Now it's my turn to say, 'Wow!' I'm sorry you had to go through this, but I'm glad you made it here. Now, I'm picking up on the letter "L," or "Lee." This is someone who's passed."

"Oh my goodness! I can't believe you just said that! My family is at the wake for Lee today!" she exclaimed.

"I'm also getting something about her being like the mother, or a mother figure," I continued, thinking how cool it was that I was able to connect.

"She was! She was a huge part of my mother-in-law's life, and was like a mother to her!"

I went on, then, to pick up on all the names of the family members, including the husband and the husband's dog, who was a real companion to him. I even went so far as to name another initial, "B," and that the message "Love, here" was for that person, though she wasn't able to validate that until she was driving home. She emailed me after she realized the "B" was for "Buddy," the name of Lee's son who was currently in the hospital with stage-four cancer.

I told Marah she had no worries. Lee was her motivation, and why we were miraculously able to squeeze her in for the extremely quick half-hour session. Her motivating factor was Lee. She wanted everyone to know she was still around, that the afterlife was real, and that she loved them all. I also believe this session changed Marah's life, and will by extension alter the beliefs of her husband.

I was finishing up, and both my body and Marah's body filled with goose bumps, validation that her loved one was present. She was so amazed that she continued asking questions and promising as she put on her coat, "I will hurry! I know you have another client waiting! I am just so excited! And can I have that paper? The one where you wrote everything down? I want to take it home! My husband will never believe any of it!"

"Absolutely, I replied. It's all yours," and I handed her the paper that had numerous psychic hits written on it. "Just as long as you promise to spread 'Alodia's' love." She'd remembered Lee's real name was Lodia or Alodia, which explained the strange names I received when I originally wrote "Lee" on the paper.

Motivation can be intuitive. It can be gentle nudges from the other side. In fact, in Marah's case, it was such a strong and powerful force that she even argued with her husband about it!

Drive

Is the motivation enough to create the desire to manifest greatness? Motivation of any type gets you going. Does it have the staying power to keep you going? That really depends on how strong the drive or the need is compared to the value of what you will gain. In Marah's case, she couldn't deny the desire to come in and see me. Every circumstance is different. The need for food is key to our survival, but would that create the urge to manifest greatness? Probably not; merely surviving is not enough to force that urge. However, if you are truly motivated to cure cancer, manifesting greatness is probably going to rank pretty high on your list.

Utilizing the motivation to get stuff moving is not always the next step. Take the cure for cancer. We all, I think it's safe to say, would love to have a cure for cancer. Does this mean we are all scientists looking for that cure? Or do we all raise money on a regular basis to combat cancer? Do we all volunteer in a cancer ward or work with terminally ill cancer patients? The simple answer is no. This does not make us terrible people. It simply means the desire to cure the disease is not influenced strongly enough internally to motivate us to be the one to cure it. It doesn't mean we haven't been affected or haven't lost someone to the disease, or that we don't want a cure. It's just not what we are meant to do at this point in our lives. Thankfully, others do possess the motivating factors and are working on that cure as we speak.

Being motivated is definitely one of the necessities to manifesting greatness. Not everyone will reach their peak. Most of us will simply survive, enjoying the little things in life. There is nothing wrong with appreciating the day-to-day events. Just know that it is in our greatness that we shine and ultimately experience joy. Our motivations are there; we just have to make sure they are strong enough that we no longer want to merely settle.

• •

WEEK 26 EXERCISE:

IT'S TIME TO GET MOTIVATED!

We all want to accomplish things. Whether menial tasks or monumental feats, accomplishment makes us feel good. On this first day of the week, make a list of your clear motivators. Include any factors that you feel have, in the past or currently in the present, motivated you to do something or to change something. Then write down what they motivated you to do.

For the second day, you're making another list. Record potential motivations for your future. For example, you want to be able to buy a new car, so that's motivation for you to work more hours or look for a different job. Or possibly you want to look "buff," so you're motivated to go back to the gym. Be sure to include anything you can think of, no matter how extraordinary it may seem.

The following day, write in your journal any motivators that did not work. For example, sometimes your significant other calling you fat will motivate you to go on a diet. More often than not, though, your motivation will wane, leaving you with a worse feeling than when you started. Or the desire for new clothes was outweighed by the discontinued motivation to work two jobs. You can include any failed motivators you remember.

On the fourth day, you're going to step into the role of reporter. Find out what motivates others. Ask your friends, your family, your coworkers, and even your teachers or classmates which motivations have worked for them and which haven't. Include whether they were able to accomplish their goals or tasks due to their motivating factors.

The next day, look at all of your lists. Are these short-term, goal-oriented motivations? Like buying new clothes? Or are they strong enough to continue on as motivating factors for manifesting greatness? Either way is totally fine, just note which they are.

On the sixth day, motivate others! What can you do to help others achieve their goals? First, find out what their goals are. Remember, on the fourth day you asked what motivates others. Put that information to good use today! Help them out! Make sure you use positive motivation rather than negative motivation, or it will most certainly cause you grief.

On the last day, decide whether you want to manifest greatness. What does your gut tell you? Are you ready to maximize your potential? Write down what you think your potential is, and if you've already begun reflecting on the possibility or not. Do you think you can reach your greatness? One way or another, buckle up! By reading this book you've already bought your ticket! And you're in for a fun ride!

Motivating

"I am motivated by _____**."**

✍ ☺

. . . .

What We Want and What We Need

We all want to succeed. None of us set out to accomplish failure. There is a distinct difference, however, between what we want and what we need. Do you need to manifest greatness in order to have a happy life? No, but you do need to manifest your greatness in order to experience true joy. This kind of joy trumps everything else, and has a lasting effect on you and those around you.

Determining what you want versus what you need is not essential. It doesn't have to be a deciding factor in making decisions as you live your life. Your wants and needs are really tied up together, in a festive dance of longing. Experiencing the cravings and the desires is what keeps you alive. These yearnings keep you focused and on task and excited that there is more out there in the universe than what you currently have.

Without the excitement of possibility, there would be no want. Alternatively, without the excitement of possibility there *would* still be need. Need is different from want because it is detrimental to our survival. But there are levels of need. At its very basic core, we need food, water, and shelter to survive. The amount or type is different for everyone, but the need is real. Without needs, we couldn't continue to exist.

Money, money, money, money

I did a phone reading recently for Kurt. It was only a half-hour session, so we quickly got to the fundamental root of why he was looking for guidance. He needed money. Not just because he wanted to go shopping or go on vacation. He needed money to pay his mortgage and buy groceries. Kurt was terrified he was going to lose his home, as his mortgage was past due. I consoled him by telling him that I psychically was seeing that he would be staying in his current house, able to take care of his elderly father, and would be okay. This was the first level of need.

Next, he wanted to make sure he would have the money to pay for his child's next semester of college. The tuition was due, and Kurt didn't have it. Again, I was able to comfort him by telling him I truly did see his child graduating, no problem. That was level two. He didn't need that money to survive, but he needed it to provide the education for his child that they'd worked so hard for.

Now, what was interesting was when I told him I saw him adding something to his current career to get it stimulated again, financially, he immediately reverted back to being sad, exclaiming, "I already tried leaving my sales job! It didn't work! I just came back to it! I don't want to change again!"

Now, because Kurt was so wrapped up in crisis mode, he didn't realize I had said he needed to add something rather than stop what he was currently doing. I said, "In fact, you may have already just added it."

It hit him then, that in his need to provide for himself, his father, and his child, he had already added medical-supply sales to his pharmaceutical sales. "Oh, I just did that. All right, good."

My client had experienced a slight shift between what he needed and what he wanted. Kurt knew he had to make things work financially, but at the same time he knew he didn't want to change his career again. This was just fine, as what he was doing was going to work for him. You can see how easily the two intertwine—need and want.

As it happens, we don't always know what we want. Occasionally, it's because what we want is influenced by what we need. Take money. We all want it, because we all need it. But do we all want the same amount? Do we want the things we can buy with it? Do we want it just to count it? Most of the time there are more in-depth reasons behind what we desire. When we are looking toward manifesting greatness, we have to see beyond what's needed to get to what we want for our soul and our spirit to make our heart sing.

• •
WEEK 27 EXERCISE:
DO WE REALLY NEED IT?

Spend this first day examining what you really need out of life. Record everything you don't think you can live without. Include absolutely all you feel you need! Don't leave anything out.

On the next day, revise your list of needs! That cell phone you wrote down may feel like a necessity, but is it more of a luxury? Not everyone has one, and they can still make it through the day. Growing up I never had one; they weren't even in existence. It's okay to keep it on your list, however, if you feel it is a legitimate necessity. Possibly, you just need a very basic one, not a smartphone. But it is feasible, if you're like me, that you do a lot of work on your smartphone, which does put it in that need column. Again, this is about you and what needs you have.

The third day, think about what you want. If you have always longed to be a tightrope walker in the circus, then write it down! Maybe you want a new house or more money. Be sure to be detailed with your wants as well. It is okay to want.

On the fourth day, yes, you are going to revise your wants! Do you really want to race in the Indy 500? Or was that just something you thought was cool? Weed out the things that really don't matter to you at all, or that you would never try and attain.

The next day, it's time to go over both the need list and the want list. Have you been redundant? If you said you wanted more money, was it because you wanted to buy a horse? If "Buy a horse" is on your list, get rid of "More money." The money is the means to an end, or the way to get to your result.

With manifesting, it is not about how you will get what you want to bring into your life; it's about the act of putting the thought into the universe to convey, in some way, that which you want.

During the rest of the week, revise your lists. Pare them down to the goals or achievements or desires that you really wish to attain. Remember, there is no right or wrong list; this is specific to you and your life.

Manifesting

"I have everything I need."

Chapter 6

What's Challenging You?

(WEEKS 28–32)

What's Holding You Back?

There is nothing written in stone or even on paper that proclaims you are not allowed to succeed. No one has the power to tell you now, as an adult, that you aren't allowed to manifest greatness. You have the potential for greatness; you need only access it. You are in control, even if it doesn't always feel that way.

Thinking outside of the box

Believing in who you are and what you are capable of will help you break free from any restraints that are self-imposed. That can be hard if you're constantly letting your peers put you down, or worse, if you're continually labeling yourself in unflattering ways. Exploring your various talents will offer you the proof that you are worthy. Anne Brontë wrote, "…all our talents increase in the using, and every faculty, both good and bad, strengthens by exercise…" Stay away from the unwarranted negativity and reiterate the positives for all they're worth!

Do you have any negative beliefs about yourself? Do you impose boundaries on what you can or can't do? Do you limit your desires because you believe you are not valuable? Do you distance yourself from fun because you feel it's frivolous? Unfortunately, I'd be willing to bet you answered yes to at least a few if not all four of these questions. That is quite common.

We hesitate to break out of our box for fear that we will lose our identity or that we will lose the tangibles we already possess. Without any concrete evidence of our greatness, we weave a pitiful story about ourselves. It's the intangibles, however, that are actually the most important. Our values, our beliefs, our talents—these are significant. But it's also the intangibles that we can't touch or hold in our hands.

Are you confident with who you are? Very few of us can say with a straight face that we are. We usually find something wrong: "I'm too fat," or "I'm too dumb," or "I don't have any skills," or "I can't do that," or "Nobody wants me," or "I don't know how I'm ever going to be able to accomplish anything."

A slight shift in perspective can project a different set of ideals, thereby giving you the perception that your shape is awesome, or you're smart, or you have all the skills you need to do what you're doing, or you can do that, and people want you, and you will accomplish whatever you set out to do.

Which view would you rather take? In the first, you are limiting yourself. You have created a negative cycle that will be very hard to escape from. In the second, you have opened the way to achievement by paving it with positive energy. That negative cycle will always be responsible for holding you back; resistance to change is at its core. The positive spin creates space for confidence to blossom. It allows your talents and your abilities to bloom in full force for others to admire and emulate.

Square peg, round hole

We learn to lose confidence as we grow up. Being criticized is one of the main causes of a lack of self-esteem. If someone tells you you're not good enough or you should take a back seat to another person, often enough you'll start believing this is true for every aspect of your life. Did a family member start this cycle? A teacher? Usually it's pounded into us at a young age. Alternatively, positive affirmations or direction can instill a feeling of self-assurance.

Believing any of the unwarranted criticisms that have been directed at you can put a damper on your ability to live your dreams or get started manifesting greatness. Having someone tell you what you can or can't do based on their own world perspective will never match up entirely to your own personal viewpoint. If we allow the wool to be pulled over our eyes, or the veil to block our own vision, we begin accepting their ideas instead of nurturing our own. When asked what the number-one reason keeping people from living their dreams is, best-selling author Mike Dooley, in his book *Manifesting Change*, states that the answer is simple: "Not understanding the nature of our reality, who we are, and the actual mechanics that bring about change."

It's hard to move forward if you're feeling like a square peg in a round hole. A central barrier to reaching any goals or advancing is that feeling of not quite fitting in. This often happens when attempting something new—social situations, sports, career, relationships, and even performing on stage. If you push the square peg into the round hole hard enough, it will either break or you will lose your edges. Those edges are what make us unique, and what make us feel special. Now, all that's left is the discomfort that's created from feeling out of place. It's essential that you are comfortable in whatever situation you find yourself. Otherwise, forward progression will inevitably stop. And, like constant critique, the more you find yourself in this position, the less confident you will be to try something new again.

Aspiration, not perspiration

If you aspire to nothing, you will be nothing; you will create nothing. You need to want to do or generate or be something. This, then, may be the biggest deterrent there is—lack of desire to accomplish anything. Not only will this hold you back, but it will also create a lack of space needed to breathe, and eventually you will feel useless.

Yet another roadblock to success is the belief that someone else will make everything better. It is the idea that there's someone else who's in charge of your life. The reality is you own your life; you make things happen. You are the only one who can succeed for you. No one else can make that happen. It's up to you to determine what you want to have or what you want to possess. Otherwise, *you* will be the one holding you back—no one else is to blame.

There is nothing more incredible than coming into your own. Acknowledging that you are responsible for developing your life into what you want will open you up to a new way of being. It is incredibly gratifying when you realize that you have every tool in your personal toolkit to manifest greatness. Get ready to take off.

• •

WEEK 28 EXERCISE:

DO YOU BELIEVE IN YOURSELF?

On the first day, surprise! You're going to make a list! Write down anything you feel that's been holding you back in any way. Include in this list everything that's been obvious, as well as those hidden barriers that may now be coming to light. Include people here, also. If there's anyone in your life that you feel has been holding you back in some way, write their name down. Remember: this is your list. Nobody else has to see it, so be honest.

The next day, go back over your list. Are there any areas that you can easily remove? You may find that just by acknowledging the blockage is there in the first place, you may be well on your way to getting rid of it. If there are any people in your life who continually hold you back or restrain you, it may be time to cut them out of your life. Is there someone who causes you more stress or more grief than happiness? It may be time to revisit whether you need such people in your life, or whether you have room for them. Put some real thought into this process and know that it may take you a while.

On the third day, revise your list. Now, what's still holding you back? What do you have left after cutting out everything on day two? Pay special attention to anything that you might be holding on to, or that you may not be ready to get rid of. These are the ones that may be the most difficult. These are the ones that are caused by a belief we may have learned. Write them down.

The fourth day you will spend writing down everything you've always wanted to try and anything you've always wanted to do but never felt quite good enough or never created the opportunity to allow yourself to do. You can make it as extreme or as simple as you want. If flying an airplane is something you've never done but always felt would be fun, go ahead and write that down. If trying the new restaurant in town has been something you've been longing to do but were shy about, go ahead and list that as well. Include in your journal all the things people may have told you that you couldn't do that you want to do. Once you're done writing everything down, go back and put a star next to those things you feel you'd really like to try soon.

Now comes the fun part. On the fifth day you are going to do something crazy. You are actually going to go out into the world and try something you may never have thought you could do. This doesn't mean that you can go out and drive a race car today (unless you know somewhere that offers training for this). But it does mean that you can go play on the swings at the local park and not worry or feel uncomfortable about what people will say. Sometimes it's the simple things in life that we put off doing because we're afraid of what people will think about us. Today you're not going to worry about it! As long as it's not going to hurt someone and it's not illegal, it is your chance to enjoy!

For the remainder of the week, you're going to continue to do the things that you've written down. Set out to accomplish things you may never have done had it not been for your lists. Chances are you won't complete everything and there are many things on the list that will take a lot more time and effort to achieve, but this is your beginning; this is your new start. What are you waiting for?

Manifesting

"I am responsible for my own life."

. . . .

Working Through Your Fears

Ann Marie is a forty-something wife and the mother of two beautiful girls. She's able to work a full-time job and take care of her household. She's brave and courageous and is well respected at her job. But, she came to see me because she has to do a presentation at work and she is afraid to speak in front of everyone. She has to address sixty people about something she's already implemented in her job and knows like the back of her hand, but she's scared she won't remember what she has to say and won't be able to speak up.

Within about five minutes of first meeting each other, we figured out why. Her father, a single dad working hard to provide for his two children, taught her that she should be quiet, that "children should be seen and not heard." She also grew up with everyone, people she never knew before, staring at her. You see, she has a twin sister, and they always had the same haircut and dressed identically. People continually did a double take, unintentionally embarrassing Ann Marie and causing her to try and hide.

These two repeated situations made her feel uncomfortable whenever anyone watched her and kept her from being able to speak up or voice her opinion about anything. By restructuring those subconscious thoughts, and allowing her to instead look back at others, which she enjoys doing, and encouraging her to use her voice, she is getting some of that confidence back. It was her life training that contributed to the fear she was experiencing.

Like the Babe said

Fear has a way of a holding you back from being able to do anything. It can cause immobility and stress. Fear also has a way of creating anger and frustration. When you make choices out of fear, it constricts you. Fear makes demands on us. It teaches us not to speak up, as in Ann Marie's case, and it tries to convince us that anything we want shouldn't be ours.

Babe Ruth said, "Don't let the fear of striking out hold you back." Babe, one of baseball's greats, nailed it. You have to go for it! When you make a decision out of fear, you are lending credence to your idea that you're not strong enough to be in control of your own life. When you don't have faith that you can actually hit that ball on your own, you give up any possibility of reaching greatness.

For fear's sake

We also fear independence. Many people have a difficult time being alone. This creates a need to stay with somebody who may not be the ideal match. This fear also can create a false idea that we are responsible for taking care of people who dismiss us only so that we don't have to be by ourselves. This can carry through to a work environment where we are afraid to perform a task alone, because we fear we are not good enough to do it correctly. It challenges our independence and makes us question whether we even know what we're doing.

Have you ever done something just because someone wanted you to? Have you ever given up something you wanted in order to make someone else happy? Have you ever done something you didn't want to do for the sake of pleasing someone else?

Occasionally we do for others because it's in our nature; we want to make others happy. More often than not, though, we do these things because we're afraid to disappoint them. Disappointment from others reflects back, and we absorb it. It makes us feel smaller. It makes us feel bad, especially if the person asking us to do something really needs our help. When we do for others, we feel an incredible sense of benevolence, which is something we usually value. We experience joy through helping others, but that joy is interrupted if it prevents us from pursuing our own dreams or own goals.

Being afraid of actual objects can also disrupt our path to greatness. Phobias like being afraid of heights can really put a damper on your desire to hang-glide. Or being scared of the water will absolutely deter you from swimming with dolphins. Usually there's a reason that we're afraid of something. If you can get to the heart of the matter or the initial sensitizing event, there's a good chance you will be able to abolish your fear. If you are debilitated by anxiety, it would be a good idea to contact a therapist. If you feel you may be able to control your worry, then let's go!

Fear takes away from our journey. Apprehension interrupts our flow and makes it more difficult to continue down our path. Merely stopping in order to avoid something can cause us to change direction or go off course. Banishing those fears will give you a leg up on manifesting greatness.

● ●

WEEK 29 EXERCISE:
WHO'S AFRAID?

Everyone is afraid of something. It's a given. How you handle your fear is what will eventually get you to the next level. On the first day, list as many of your fears as you can think of. Include here any objects, ideas, or even events or situations that scare you. If you're afraid to sleep on one side of the bed versus the other, write that down. If you're afraid of snow, include that as well. If spiders make you freak out, write it down.

The next day, separate that list into ideas, events, and objects. An idea may be panic of presenting in front of people. An event may be skiing or swimming, and obviously objects could include spiders or dogs.

On the third day, put those fears in order from the one you're least afraid of to the one that scares you the most. As you review your list, you may find that there are things you've written down that no longer apply to you. Go ahead and cross those off. For instance, if you're no longer afraid of spiders, put a line through that one.

On the fourth day, you're going to work through your fears. If you need the help of a friend, enlist them because today is the day you're going to get over one of the things that has held you back.

Hypnosis is a common remedy for ridding yourself of stress. Self-hypnosis can help you by either recognizing the initial sensitizing event or changing the way your subconscious feels about something. For the purposes of this exercise, you are going to pick whatever you're afraid of that you want to conquer.

Find a comfortable chair to sit in where you won't be restricted or interrupted in any way. Close your eyes and take a deep breath. As you inhale, allow a feeling of relaxation to begin flowing down from the top of your head on the way down to the tips of your toes. Now hold your left arm out in front of you, keeping your eyes closed the whole time. Begin counting down in your mind, starting with the number 100. You'll find that your arm will begin to get tired. It may be getting so tired that you feel it touching down on to your body in front of the chair. When it does, just allow it to rest like your right arm is.

With every number, allow your body to become more and more relaxed. With every number, feel yourself slipping away, going deeper and deeper and deeper still. As you continue to count down, all the way down, the numbers may begin to fade. As the numbers fade away, you become more and more relaxed. Once you feel you're totally relaxed—so relaxed in fact that even though you know you could open your eyes anytime, you know you no longer need to—go ahead and give your eyes a little test and see how comfortably closed they stay.

Good. Now, imagine you're in front of a staircase. Imagine that the staircase has ten steps leading down. In a moment imagine I'm going to begin counting down, starting with the number 10. With every step as you walk down those stairs, become more and more relaxed. Ten, nine, eight, seven, six, five, four, three, almost there, two, and one. Down at the bottom of the stairs now. As you step off, you enter into a beautiful meadow. The grass is crisp and clean, and all the colors are clearer than ever before.

As you look into the meadow, you see that there's a blanket lying on the ground; make your way over to the blanket. The blanket looks warm and inviting, comfortable. You easily make your way down onto the blanket and remove your shoes, your toes in the grass, grounding yourself. Feel the strength rising up from the earth traveling through your toes up and into your legs, your knees, your thighs, and your hips. Allow the energy to travel, all the way up through your abdomen into your chest and your back, up through your shoulders and out your arms, down to your fingertips, and out. That beautiful earth energy moves up through your neck, across your face and your mouth and your eyes and finally out the top of your head.

Now imagine in front of you is a movie screen. As you watch the screen, you can see it rewinding, taking you back to a time and a place where you were so happy, so excited. Watch as the image appears on the screen and you see yourself laughing, keyed up even. Allow yourself to luxuriate in that feeling. Are you alone? Are you inside? Outside? Are there others with you? Are you at home? What are you wearing? If you're with someone else, what are they wearing?

Go back another minute in time, back to when you first started laughing, right before you got excited. What were you doing? Good. Feel that feeling again, the feeling of laughter taking over. See yourself on the screen as you light it up, smiling and laughing.

Now, in the bottom left corner of your screen, you see something you are afraid of. Something that's been holding you back from moving forward. As it begins to grow in size, this apprehension turns into a big black blob and starts spreading across the screen, making its way all the way across. But, now this is important, your image is there, your smile, your laughter! The fear is diminishing. The big black blob is beginning to shrink! Your image gets even bigger, now, and the laughter is louder. Your smile is shining light, diamonds sparkling off the screen. You hear the sound of laughing and realize it's amplified; there are others laughing with you! Your fear, your apprehension, the big black blob is getting even smaller now, melting almost into a puddle in the bottom right corner of the screen. You watch in amazement as your laughter gets so amplified that you can almost see it blowing off of the screen. The black puddle of fear is now dripping off the screen, down into the earth to be recycled into positive energy. You are no longer sharing your life or the screen image with that fear. It's no longer a part of you. It has been replaced with laughter and excitement. Pure joy is now in its place, and there is not enough room to ever let it back in!

Stay here, with your eyes closed, for as long as you'd like.

When you are ready, I am going to count to five and you will open your eyes, perfectly refreshed and ready to continue your day. One, take a deep breath in; two, moving your fingers and toes; three, take another deep breath in; four, feel yourself back in your body; and five. Open your eyes, perfectly refreshed, and filled with positive energy!

For the rest of the week, do this self-hypnosis exercise with any other fears you have listed that may be holding you back. You can even repeat it if you need reinforcement on a particular fear.

You are a strong and capable being! Enjoy it!

Manifesting

"My old fear of _____

is no longer holding me back."

✍ ☺
. . . .

Respect

Respect. Aretha Franklin sure could sing about it, and her signature song has become an anthem; young and old alike belt it out at parties, at karaoke, at bars, and in clubs. The thing about respect is it goes both ways. You have to give it, and you need to make sure you receive it.

Respect yourself

As children we are taught, one hopes, to respect our parents, and those in authority, such as teachers, firefighters, police officers, and basically our elders. I have taught my children this, and as they grow I am proud to see them adhere to these basic societal rules. However, I share another point of view with my friend Mike. We were discussing the subject while we were watching our kids play lacrosse. He said, "Respect must be earned; it cannot be commanded." Mike is a police officer. I grew up respecting the badge, as my uncle was also a cop. But I was glad to hear Mike say it's not automatic; it doesn't come without deserving it. And I absolutely agree with him.

There's more to respect. The basic definition of *respect* means to hold someone or something in high esteem or regard, or to admire or defer to them. We easily look up to others as valuable contributors in society, and we bend in deference to them, including many of the people we've listed as successful from the "Who Do You Think Is Great?" exercise in chapter 1. Probably most important, however, is respecting and having respect for ourselves. This means being kind to others, being considerate, and keeping our ego in check. If we can't respect who we are and what we do, how will we ever reach any level of greatness?

Ego and respect are poles apart even though they frequently become enmeshed. When you respect others, you honor them by listening to their opinions or their concerns. You thoughtfully appreciate and offer consideration when they need your help or even when they want to teach you something. Ego doesn't allow for honor; in fact, it's quite the opposite. When you listen to others from an egotist point of view, your way will always be the right way. It becomes impossible to learn because you think you know everything or can do it better than someone else.

There will always be someone, somewhere, who will be smarter, or more athletic, or more philanthropic, or more advanced, or more medically inclined, or more talented than you. Acting from a place of ego rather than respect restricts you from moving forward. A tiny dose of humility will help you if you feel your ego is taking off on its own!

In my line of work, I regularly experience a lack of respect. I always tell people I will not try and make them approve of what I do, but I do anticipate a modicum of respect for who I am. Simply said, I am a good person and treat others respectfully. I am a caring parent and thoughtful toward my friends. I also happen to be psychic.

Recently, there was a three-quarter-page article about me in the newspaper. It was a wonderful write-up that I hope answered many questions people often have about psychics in general and specifics about what I do and how I work. After this article came out, I was inundated with phone calls and emails requesting my services. I also received one phone call and one email from two different anonymous people, or perhaps I should say chickens. The "private caller" said, "You are the devil. You are working with demons. You are the demon child. You are the demon!" The email carried this sentiment as well, but added, "You are a scam artist. You scam 'intelligent' people. You are disgusting." As pleasant as that was, I chose to ignore them both.

Judge and jury

We judge others when we don't understand them or when we haven't been in their position. The old adage "Never judge someone until you have walked a mile in their shoes" says it perfectly. With judgment comes disrespect. Unless you are in an extraordinary position, don't judge! I find every time I judge someone, I end up quickly in the same type of situation. Remember that thing about karma; it will come back around!

Respecting yourself and others is crucial as you gain momentum toward greatness. It's a fundamental necessity and reality that to manifest greatness you have to like who you are and what you're doing. Greatness will never come without respect!

· ·

We use words to describe our lives and the world we live in. We can choose to make them positive words. For this first day, write down every single positive word you can about yourself. Do not limit yourself to the first five things that pop into your mind; you're better than that! Dig deep, the deeper the better.

On the second day, use those words positively. Throughout the entire day, create positive sentences using each of the words. For example, if you said you were a good writer, your sentence can simply be, "I AM a good writer." Use your own vernacular, something that works for you, but make it real. Repeat your sentences throughout the day. Trust your words! Respect yourself enough to believe what you're saying.

The next day, write down qualities you respect in yourself. Possibly you will be including some descriptions from the positive words list. Are you generous with your time, your money, or your emotions? Do you share your natural talents or gifts freely? Have you always been the first in line to help others? Be sure to record everything, from being caring and helping animals to putting together an effort to feed the homeless to being a great host or hostess. It's not always about contributions or donations to others; it's also how you handle yourself and accomplish things in your personal life.

On the following day, it's time to acknowledge qualities in others that you respect. This is not the space just to list people you've previously recognized as successful; rather, now is the time to record anything you respect about anyone other than yourself. Take care to really write down everything you can think of, including the person's name and how they display or utilize the specific qualities you are recording.

The fifth day should be spent comparing the lists with a very nonjudgmental view. Write down what qualities you respect in yourself that you've also listed about others. Are the lists very similar? Are they extremely different? Are you repeating most of what you've written off both lists, the qualities in you and others? Don't question it, just write it down.

On the sixth day, review what you've written over the last few days. Are there qualities you respect in others that you didn't list as ones you already possess? Which of these traits do you believe would help you gain more respect for yourself if they were yours? Which are less important for you to possess in order to garner respect?

The last day of the week, decide which one or two qualities you are going to strive to achieve. Which one(s) would help you to respect yourself more? Once you've figured this out, it's time to determine how you can change or add that trait to your life. Devise an actual plan that will enable you to incorporate that quality. It may be something simple like speaking up on someone else's behalf or not spending the extra ten dollars on something you don't need. Whatever you come up with, go ahead and put it into action. Be sure to check in with yourself over the next few weeks and note whether adding that quality increased your respect for yourself or not.

Manifesting

"I respect myself because _____."

✍ ☺

. . . .

Fear of Success

What if I said the only thing that keeps you from what you want is your own certainty that it's impossible? How about if you were able to change that? If you believed that you could succeed and actually thrive? Well, it's true. The first step is to trust.

In order to grow and expand our consciousness and our world, we need to stay open and adapt to opportunities. If we are scared to change, we hold ourselves back. Reaching the top of anything brings with it a new point of view. This alters our perspective and means we have to adjust the way we think and look at things. This new viewpoint can shake our stability and really rock our world.

Flipping out

I had a hypnosis/coaching client come in a while back. Jennifer was there because she was a cheerleader, and she needed to be able to do a back handspring into a back tuck. In order to move up to the next cheer team, a more advanced team, she not only had to have her tumbling pass but also to be good at it. She'd learned to do the tumbling already, so she and I both knew she was capable. It should have been simple, but instead, every time she was asked to try the tumbling sequence she'd flip out, and not in a good way.

We discussed why she thought she was having a hard time with it. "Are you scared you'll fall and get hurt?" I asked.

"I'm not sure. I guess," Jennifer replied.

"Okay, well, let's get going!" I told her and we began the hypnosis session.

As it turns out, she was not really afraid of hurting herself. Rather, she was afraid of succeeding. If she landed her tumbles, she would have been promoted up to the next team. That meant she would be leaving her friends on her current team. It also signified she'd be performing on a higher level; there would be more chance for her to mess up! Jennifer was afraid to succeed, so she held herself back.

No guarantees

What if you were guaranteed not to fail? Would you attempt to succeed? Jennifer was afraid of victory. She didn't want to leave her teammates and also felt by succeeding she would be setting herself up for failure. Walt Disney said, "All our dreams can come true—if we have the courage to pursue them." If we change our belief about the ability to succeed, we can conquer our fear of success!

Quicksand

Fear of success can show up for many reasons. One reason, I found out, can have a huge impact on happiness. As with most fears, being afraid of success revolves around change. I did a workshop on manifestation. I taught my students that it was their option to soar to greatness. One asked me why. "Why should I? What if I am comfortable where I am?"

"Listen," I said. "It's up to you if you want to remain as you are. If you truly are content where you are, that's great. If not, and you feel stagnant, or like you're slugging through quicksand, it's time to break free from your old beliefs and allow yourself to shoot for success."

This student—and I've come across many others like her—was afraid to change what she was used to. She grew up believing she would be middle class, an average wife and mother, and she was supposed to be content to stay there. She didn't want to change and ignored that she was sinking. Again, if that's what makes you happy, you are fine. But if you've taken the opportunity to come to a class to be successful in manifesting more for yourself, then you are not in a place you wish to stay any longer.

A friend and I were talking about finances. "It may not be perfect, but it's what I know. Everything will be fine. I never really believed I could have anything else. Wouldn't being successful change my life? Won't it disrupt my family? That's pretty scary. Do you really think I could have more?" she asked.

Absolutely—she could have it all. Being a partner in a wonderful relationship and having a family that you enjoy is success in and of itself. But if there is an inkling of wanting something more, something to add to what you already have, then you need to set your fear aside and go for it. So often, we've grown up learning that "life is hard" or "that's just the way it is" or "we'll always be broke." We've learned to believe it. Our parents always said it, so it must be true. We are allowed to change our thoughts. Imagine saying, "Life is great!" or "We can change it for the better" or "Financial prosperity is ours!"

Along the same lines, I've run across people who are living their lives and are happy. They are afraid to reach or search for something to get them closer to their own personal greatness for fear that success will ruin what they already have. They don't believe they could have more and increase their enjoyment. And they're right! It will change, but the opportunity to advance in life can absolutely outweigh the fear of success.

We all have something we are fearful of. It can be very difficult to get over this worry, especially if it's debilitating or incapacitating. Luckily, a fear of success is easily broken up when we are able to achieve something positive that we may have been previously afraid of.

Fear does not have to control how close to greatness you allow yourself to get. It also doesn't have to hold you back from being able to manifest. This is part of your birthright. It's what is expected of you. Believing this will help propel you on your way to creating and living a life that has everything to do with your purpose here on earth, and by extension assist you in manifesting greatness. We have only a short time in this lifetime to achieve our greatness—make it count!

• •

WEEK 31 EXERCISE:
FEAR NO MORE!

Make a list of anything about success that you are apprehensive about. List the basics. For example, Jennifer was afraid she wouldn't have friends on her new team. Also, write down your learned beliefs. These are ideas or opinions you have formed over the years or possibly learned from your parents or family. Include here any limiting behaviors you have developed as well.

On the next day, share one of your fears with a friend. Make it someone who you trust—someone who will listen to you. Be honest with them.

On the third day, it's time to be the healer. Ask your friend if they are afraid in any way of success. It may be they are used to their life the way it is and apprehensive that any change would disrupt what they have, for the worse. Listen to your friend's thoughts. Do you fear the same thing? What can you tell your friend to help them better themselves and make the leap toward greatness?

For the next couple of days, play "What if?" In other words, if you were to set your aim toward success, what would happen? Maybe you've been afraid of asking someone on a date because even if this person did say yes, you are scared you won't live up to their expectations. Write down what you imagine would happen. Does it make sense? Does it frighten you?

On the sixth day, do something that scares you! You don't have to make a huge leap. I'm not telling you to go out and quit your job because you want something better (unless you have something else already lined up). But if that's what you need to do to pursue your idea of success, then take the first step. Look into what options you'd have. Start your research into what jobs are available, or even put together your résumé and begin sending it out! Take that step to get past your fear!

The final day, go over that list of fears you've written down. Say each one out loud, one at a time. Sometimes, we mask fear with other emotions. As you voice every one, pay attention to whether you experience any other emotion. Do you feel angry? Sad? Happy? Irritated? Take it a little deeper; is there a reason you're feeling that way? Recognizing what's actually going on can get you that much closer to understanding and vanquishing your fear of success!

Manifesting

"I am successful in so many ways;
fear does not hold me back."

Improving Your Outlook

Believing in greatness changes your life. The mere act of having faith that there is something there—something outside of you as well as within—that can be so amazing, so incredible, will open you up and let the goodness in life flow through you. Not every piece of coal becomes a diamond; like you, the coal has to be formed in order to shine like a diamond because of, rather than in spite of, the crushing weight of change. Without the restraints of doubt holding you back, nothing can stop you.

Brilliance

My husband said to me the other day, "It's a dangerous thing to have a vocabulary." What he meant was: the more we know, the more we have to change. If we can put words to something to describe it, then we have to be ready to acknowledge it. Strictly speaking, we don't need to store up our words to avoid having to address our dilemmas or our dreams and act rashly without forethought. Rather, we should let them percolate so we have intentional contemplation behind our imminent actions.

If we were a "dumb" society, living within the lines and accepting whatever misery or monotony came our way would be totally acceptable. But we are lucky. We live in a society filled with brilliance and energy. We have the ability and the wherewithal to create something spectacular of ourselves. It's the knowledge that we can advance that helps us improve our outlook.

We've learned how to tap into the universal energy that is abundant around us and within us. Using our intuition, we've opened ourselves to new possibilities and a new psychic language that we may never have utilized before. We understand how respecting ourselves will only aid in our desire for success and that fear will set us back. If you were to stop now, you'd already be further on your path to greatness than you've ever been before, and that would be fine. Except, now it's your turn. It's your turn to figure out what you really want. It is also your time to shine for all to see—to bring forth the brilliance that is knocking at your spiritual door in celebration.

Previously, it may have felt that greatness was out of your purview. You might have been assuming you would only read this book to pass the time or to see what others did to accomplish their goals. Still, it's hard to deny the changes that are taking place in the way you think and the way you view people and events in your life. You are different now, and there is no going back. What was once a skewed outlook is becoming straighter and more direct. This time, you will stick to your resolve. You are ready to no longer settle for mediocrity, but instead are willing now to strive for greatness.

Improving your outlook is a process. Manifesting greatness is no different. Transformation is not instantaneous, though so often we'd like it to be. Anything worth having or achieving is worth your time and energy to make it so. As Debbie Ford says in her book *Courage: Overcoming Fear and Igniting Self-Confidence*: "The process is a journey where we look inside ourselves and reconnect with what's always been there but often hidden—an enormous power that reconnects us with our confidence and our courage."

Rose-colored glasses

Many people suggest that looking at the world through rose-colored glasses will stop you from seeing and realizing what's really going on. I say to heck with that! Look at the world from that rosy perspective! Believing in goodness and the boundless possibilities that are waiting for you will catapult you that much closer to your own goals. Life does not need to be lived as if it were a condition to be fixed. Rather, it should be enjoyed, and that pleasure should be shared with others.

Talking your talk is crucial to improving your outlook. Positive communications are sent out into the universe; this includes every thought you have. Imagine for a second how far your reach is. Remember that 1980s Fabergé Organics shampoo commercial? "... And they'll tell two friends, and so on, and so on, and so on ..." That is the magnitude of your words and actions. Your voice spreads to the masses. Your thoughts control your words, though, so choose them wisely!

• •

WEEK 32 EXERCISE:

TURN THAT FROWN UPSIDE DOWN!

You are already on your way to achieving your greatness! Now it's time to reframe your words and your world. Write down everything negative you find yourself saying over the next two days. Include in your list phrases like "We'll always be broke," "We aren't lucky," "I'm not good enough," "I'm ugly," and "It's always been this way."

Take your time. You might find you don't say certain phrases every day, but they're there, waiting to come out when you least expect it. Give it the two days, at least.

On the third day, it's time to rephrase what you've written. Change it up so you are living in the present instead of the past and make the statement positive. Instead of "We'll always be broke," write down "We have an abundance of money" or even "We are worthy of an abundance of money and allow it to flow into our lives." You can reframe it how you want, but make it in the present, not the past or even the future. You want it now!

The rest of the week you are going to create the perfect scenario for yourself. It's not enough to believe in the possibility of something better, of making the move toward greatness; you have to visualize what it is.

Imagine what your life would be like if you reached your pinnacle of greatness, if you manifested everything you wanted. Where would you live? Who would live with you? What would you be doing—for a career, socially, and so on? What would your bank account look like? Or would you even have a bank account? Would you be respected? If so, why? Are you helping people? Are others assisting you? Are you doing something you've always wanted to do? Or is this different or new?

Keep your journal close to you for these couple of days, so that you can be sure to add things that may pop into your mind as you feel them. Remember, Rome wasn't built in a day. Your ideal life shouldn't be either!

Manifesting

Go outside. Look around wherever you are.
See everything that is good.
Ignore anything that is not.

Write down what is good.
Look for more good.

Chapter 7

Visualizing Greatness

(WEEKS 33–36)

Using and Creating Your Own Symbols

It's straightforward, really—this idea that we receive information from some universal energy, or from our guides and our loved ones. In order for us to interpret their messages, we have to understand what they are telling us, psychically. In my book *The Book of Psychic Symbols: Interpreting Intuitive Messages*, I explain symbols as a way to express ideas or thoughts, physically or metaphysically. This organization of shapes, sounds, colors, tastes, and images form what we know to be a highly developed yet simple collection of psychic symbols. This language assists us in transcending the barriers between the physical plane in which we reside and the other side where the souls of our deceased communicate from.

As I said before, our messengers are going to communicate with us in a way we can understand. After all, they want us to recognize and interpret what they are telling us. But we have to also speak their language. Imagine going to Italy and trying to communicate with the residents there. Easy, right? Wrong! Not if you don't speak each other's language! It's the same with psychic symbols.

What happens, though, if we have a different language? What messages can we possibly interpret if we can't understand them? This is when our personal symbols become so important. These are the impressions we associate with certain things that may be different from the basic meanings that are common to many people. It is through these symbolic connections that we are able to identify with our intuition, which in turn can help us create our desired lives.

Manifesting using your own symbols is a way to personalize your creations or desires. Figuring out what your personal symbols are allows you to effectively visualize what it is you want. Having the image in your mind creates a more powerful thought. Focusing in on more than one of your images that has specific meaning coupled with the intent to manifest will be stronger than using someone else's generic version of what you want to bring into your life.

The feeling you have when evoking your psychic symbols will surpass any others during manifesting because such a feeling is coming from your own intuition and the universe as well as your heart. These feelings are more meaningful and instantaneous rather than planned-out or contrived. They are a natural part of your spirit and, if you are good at interpreting them, will make up a large part of your spiritual abilities.

Symbolic impressions are used to hasten the intuitive feelings or visions we may already have. It is not magic or sleight of hand. Learning to interpret the messages from the other side is actually logical and quite rational. And over time you will develop your symbols to enable you to receive communications from your deceased loved ones, guides, and the universe in different ways—for yourself and for others.

Lance

Recently I did a reading for Chris. He is an exceptional person who has an incredible outlook on life and his family, and I love his energy. We connected to a lot of people, both alive and deceased, and I tuned in to much of his life—past, present, and future. One of the messages I received for him was "bicycle." Now, bicycle for me is really pretty generic. It indicates someone who just started or needs to start an exercise routine. It also represents a solo journey or someone making his way on his path. This I relayed to Chris. He validated he indeed needed to start a program.

"I also feel it will prolong your life. You need to do this because you're too young to have your life cut short," I continued. "I'm also seeing Lance Armstrong. Do you know anyone named Lance? I know Lance is the bike guy, but there's more to it."

"Does it have to be a name? Can it be *lanced* or something?" he asked.

"Well, that's possible, but I definitely feel it has something specifically to do with Lance or Lance Armstrong. Besides being recently stripped of his titles, the only other connection I would imagine is Lance Armstrong had testicular cancer. So, maybe I'm off, unless you tell me you were diagnosed with cancer down below…"

He interrupted me. "It's cancer. Prostate."

Chris looked at me in awe rather than grief. He was more amazed that I had gotten that message for him than he was saddened by the cancer itself. "I know you told me so many other things already. I wasn't expecting this! That's incredible that you got that," he continued.

We continued the reading with many additional validations, but it really hit home that he could help direct his recovery and continue his fabulous life. He had been ready to say, "My life was fabulous. I've been blessed," and move on. His outlook was entirely different now. Everything on his bucket list was on its way to being checked off. By tuning in to Lance and looking beyond the bicycle connection, I was able to create and understand my new symbol for prostate or testicular cancer. This, in turn, helped another person, my client, understand he was still on a journey toward manifesting his personal greatness and his road through recovery could be guided.

I receive hundreds of questions from people near and far who ask, "What if my symbol doesn't match what you have in your book?" Or, "What if the symbol you've described means something else to me?" Or even, "What if my symbol isn't *in* your book? What do I do?" The answer's always the same. We all have personal symbols. These symbols help you to understand your messages—whether they are for you or for you to pass on to someone else. Spirit communicates in whatever way it can to get the message across to us.

Baseball

Baseball is a tricky symbol for me. If it comes up in a reading, it could indicate my client plays baseball or has a connection to the game or that the client's mother is trying to come through! That's because "baseball" is a personal symbol for me that my mom is around. She loved baseball. Every time I see a baseball diamond, I know it is her way of telling me she's helping me out. It's the same with any other personal symbol. If it's something specific for you, it's meaningful.

Being able to tune in to your personal language will help you to understand the different aspects and even the different steps you need to take to help you manifest your greatness. We always have signs or symbols that will keep us on our course. These messages allow us to focus on the actual journey rather than the mechanics of it. It's like taking a trip and not only being grateful for the destination but also appreciating everything along the way. Manifesting greatness is like that—enjoy the voyage!

• •

WEEK 33 EXERCISE:

PERSONAL SYMBOLS

Listed below are some very commonly referred-to symbols. Write them in your journal and then record what they mean to you. Also, write down anything that comes to mind when you are thinking about them. It's these little details that will enhance their symbolic meaning for you personally. You may find that your intuitive definition may be very similar to the somewhat generic one, or it may have an entirely different meaning, as did the baseball diamond for me. Whatever the case, be sure to include anything you can imagine for the symbol.

Angel	Apple
Baby	Beach
Brick wall	Car
Chicken	Clothing
Computer	Dog
Dragonfly	Earth
Eye	Flower
Food	Gun
Hammer	Hat
Light bulb	Man
Microphone	Moon
Necklace	Ocean
Oven	Radio
Ring	Rose
School	Stage
Staircase	Stop sign
Sun	Telephone
Waterfall	Woman

Work on these for the next couple of days. Again, include anything that strikes you as you are contemplating each one.

For the rest of the week, carry your journal around. Make note of any additional symbols you may have or may receive and record what they mean to you. Also, scribe how you came to think of each particular symbol. Write down where you were, what you were doing, who you were with, why you received the symbolic information (if there is a reason you can understand), and what time of day it is. Do you note any patterns? Also, do you think the symbol has to do with leading you toward your greatness?

Congratulations! You've just begun your own personal symbols journal!

Manifesting

"I trust in my symbolic language and appreciate the clarity with which the messages are sent to me."

Mind Over Matter

Our thoughts control our environment. There's no denying it. As Rhonda Byrne says in *The Secret*, "It is impossible to feel good and at the same time be having negative thoughts." If we focus on the beauty in our lives and the splendor that is available to us, we have no choice but to feel good. Imagine, right now, that you're smiling. Now, really smile. Just that smile alone changes how you feel, and can even go so far as to influence your vision of your future. You've also just added a new symbol to your life; by imagining how great your future can be, you've created a new symbol. A happy, smiling version of yourself is now one of your symbols. Manifesting your greatness will be easier now that you have a happy image in place. Incredible when you think about it!

It's the little things

On any given day, the opportunity to manifest greatness is available. Life continues, whether we focus on it or not—until it doesn't. You decide whether you want to participate. All the little things—a child's first step, a mother's joy, skiing down a mountain, sharing an ice cream soda, getting an "A" on a test, or merely hugging someone you love—these are the important moments. These are the times you want to recall over and over again from your memory. These are the simple joys in life.

When we direct our attention to all of the good in life, we automatically feel a pull—a desire to create more good. This extends out into the universe and builds the energy up for others to continue the already building momentum. If we instead send out all of the bad memories or thoughts we also carry, it would be like spreading a disease. Imagine it like a mold or a virus that spreads and permeates throughout everything, infecting it and covering it, eating away at the already established structure. Would you rather feel ill? Would it feel better to contract this virus? Or does delight sound better? Both can be viewed as a contagion. It's up to you to send it into the ether.

You know I like my chicken fried

We've all had those better days, and we have also had the ones we wish we could do over. This is life as we breathe it and experience it. We have the everyday woes that the country singers croon about. But we're also blessed with the basic pleasures. The Zac Brown Band sings in their song "Chicken Fried" about a house filled with love even though it's not much to talk about. The singer is recognizing that even though his house itself may be somewhat unsatisfying, that's not what is important. He understands it's the little things that really make up our greatness.

What would you do if you could visualize change? What if I told you that you can? Imagine you had the power to change the way your body felt, simply by visualizing it. Would you use that power? Would you take hold of it and embrace it? Or would you discard it or give it to someone else? So often, it's the intangibles we tend to dismiss. If we can't hold a medicine or we can't hold a cure, if it's not something tangible, it's hard for us to truly believe it can work. But it's possible. It's more than possible; it's been done and is still being done to this day. All it takes is good vibrations.

. . . .

WEEK 34 EXERCISE:
VISUALIZE WHAT MATTERS

You're putting your visualization power to work this week. On the first day, visualize your happiest occasions. Recall those times in your recent past as well as your distant memories. Spend at least ten minutes actually seeing them in your mind—remembering what you felt like in that time, during that moment.

On the next day, write them all down. Include every detail of each memory, allowing enough time to truly describe them.

On the third day, assign a symbol to each of your wonderful memories. What image comes to mind when you visually conceptualize your past event? Come up with a different symbolic reference for every one, so when you think of or see that symbol in the future it will automatically call up that specific event.

On the fourth day, do a mental scan over your body. What is something you'd like to change? Is there any discomfort? Now, imagine one of your symbols from the happy memories. Place that symbolic image directly over an area on your body where you are experiencing distress. Visualize that symbol permeating and spreading through your body, traveling directly to where it needs to go, pushing out any negativity or debris that no longer belongs there.

For the rest of the week, continue using your new symbols to "heal" different aspects of yourself.

Manifesting

Go outside. Search out joy. Find it in the little things and the natural beauty around you. If necessary, change your perspective. Lie down in the grass to see the individual blades of healing green or climb to the top of a building to view the incredible beauty in the treetops.

Images to Live By

Visualizing your success should be increasingly easy for you as you make your way through the book and all of the exercises. Possibly, you began this process unaware of what was available, and this has let the possibility of reaching greatness slip slowly through the cracks. Now, though, is your chance to use the images you have assimilated to change the way your path is headed. You don't have to do this if you don't want to, but at this point, why wouldn't you want to?

Learning from the mistakes

You are now beginning to see how all of the mistakes in your past, all of the missteps you may not have even recognized before taking this journey, have led you here. As cliché as it is, everything happens for a reason. You are present in this part of your life because of, not despite, your past. And because you know how imperative visualizing your greatness is, you need to adjust your way of seeing things.

In order to truly see anything, you need to really look. Understanding what we see comes from seeing all of the details. Recognizing the particulars follows through into the other aspects of your life as well and can contribute to how you attain what you desire. For instance, when you look at a dollar bill, what do you see? Do you just see the color? Do you see the writing? Do you see the shapes? Did you notice the pyramid with the eye on the top? If one of things you are hoping to manifest is an abundance of money, don't you think it would be helpful to also see what money actually looks like?

Even though you are usually not manifesting cash for the sake of having cash, it's still important to be aware of what you want so you can include all of the details. For example, does "tall, dark, and handsome" mean tall, skinny, and dark hair or tall, overweight but cute, with dark skin? The list could go on and on. It's virtually endless. The more you want to see your wishes fulfilled, the more you have to visualize exactly what it is you want.

Let it all hang out

Often, when I do hypno-coaching for weight-loss clients, I will have them visualize what they want to look like. Part of that is realizing what they actually look like now—not just what they let others see, but everything. Their first homework assignment is to stand naked in front of a mirror. When looking in the mirror, it's important to be objective. I have my clients stare at the parts of themselves they want to change. Then they have to take it one step further and imagine what they want those places on their body to actually look like. By visualizing the changes on their own body, it becomes more of a plausible metamorphosis rather than a diversion from reality.

Your visualizations have to be more than mere illusions or you'll never pull them off. Thinking you are imagining something that is impossible, or even that you are faking it, will absolutely prevent you from accomplishing what you are trying to achieve. Sometimes it takes all of your courage, inspiration, and determination to allow you to believe in your potential. Visualizing what you want your outcome to be helps bolster your belief in that potential.

• •

WEEK 35 EXERCISE:

I CAN SEE IT

On this first day, imagine something you really want to change in your life. It could be losing weight, or making more money, or even speaking with more fluency. Write down a few of these and think long and hard about them. Then decide which one you want to work on this week and write that down on a fresh page in your journal.

Visualizing takes time. To imagine all the details, you may need a frame of reference to start off. On the second day, tune in to that one thing you wish to manifest for yourself. In order to do this, study what it specifically represents. If it's about looking better in clothes, look for legitimate images that may represent what you can look like, in reality. In other words, if you are a woman who is hoping to look like you have super-long, molded legs, this is possible if you already have long legs and are 5'8". If you are 5'2" with super-short legs, this is a great desire, but even you know it can't happen. Be realistic with what you visualize. Otherwise, you will be setting yourself up to be disappointed.

On the third day, draw the visualization. What is it you are hoping to accomplish? What does it look like to you? Draw your hope, your dream of what it looks like when you have it. You can include where you are, who you're with, and what you're doing.

The next day, record why you desire what you have been working on this week. What would it do for you? Why do you feel it's necessary in your life? Write down every reason you can think of.

For the rest of the week, keep visualizing it. See it as it will be when you have it. Don't try and figure out how it will get there. Just imagine it is there already. Above all, enjoy the process!

Manifesting

"I clearly see what I have,
and I especially like _____**."**

(Fill in the blank!)

✍

• •

Realizing the Visions

Entrepreneur John Assaraf traveled around the world and discovered that, as he puts it in his book *Having It All*, "Happiness is a personal choice and not the product of anything external." Creating your life based on the vision of what you want your life to be can only be done by you. It's you who will judge whether you're happy and only you who is privy to your exact dream of what you want your life to be.

Try and try again

It is your right to realize your vision. But that doesn't mean there won't be any issues or any failures along the way. Without the failures there would be no learning. We learn from our mistakes, and they are what make attaining our dreams even more rewarding. It's how we handle the failures that affects the outcome. Keep trying. Don't ever give up. Give it your all, again. Once you've stopped trying, you might as well be dead. There's nothing left. That's why it's crucial to perceive those failures as educational. That wisdom can be utilized in your journey to exposing your greatness.

No cookie cutters here

You are on your path, exactly where you need to be. You have others who travel with you on their own journey. At times your courses will overlap and come together and provide you with the opportunity to both learn from and teach each other. Take advantage of all of these beneficial collisions. They are in your life to help you achieve your goals. Provide a stable and informative and open and generous model for your kids and any children around you, and make sure they are allowed to color outside the lines. Everyone has a different path, and it's up to each of us to assist them as they assist us in any way we can to realize their personal visions.

All of us are different. We are not cookie-cutter clones. I challenge you to find anyone who shares every like and dislike or every detailed vision of success. That's what makes us all so incredible; it's in our diversity that we come together. Encouraging others to thrive and to express themselves will also help us on our quest to manifesting greatness. And if you're anything like me, you will have many people who are not on the same page as you with your beliefs and what keeps you up at night.

Sweet dreams

About eight years ago I began having a terrible time sleeping. I knew, of course, that part of it was because I was a mother. I was so used to my children waking me in the middle of the night that I think I was kind of programmed to continue waking up, even if the kids were asleep. I was also convinced part of it was because I had to use the bathroom! But the doctors were unprepared for the other reason I wasn't getting a full seven hours.

I went to the hospital to do a sleep study. They hooked me up to a whole bunch of wires with sticky electrodes all over my head and my body. I didn't think there was any way I would be able to sleep. Well, I was right and wrong. I thought I slept through the night, but apparently I didn't. In the meeting with the doctor after being woken up at 5:30 am, I was asked if I had a good night's sleep.

"Yes. I wasn't woken up. I think any messages I was getting were just whispered or something, because I stayed asleep!" I answered in shock.

"I hate to break it to you, but you actually woke up an average of fifty-two times per hour," the doctor told me.

"Wow, I didn't realize that! I wasn't getting woken up last night though."

"I'm afraid you have sleep apnea. We're going to have to get you set up with a CPAP machine to help you breathe properly at night. What did you mean when you said you didn't get woken up? Are you talking about your kids?"

"No, I'm talking about the dead people," I answered, as though he'd just asked me if I wanted milk or cream for my coffee. I regularly experienced visits in the middle of the night until I put the kibosh on it and started protecting myself at night before I go to bed.

"Excuse me? I think the lack of sleep has caused you to hallucinate, so it's a good thing we are getting you that CPAP machine!" he answered, and I knew there was no convincing him.

It didn't matter what the doctor thought. I didn't need to convince him that I was getting visited by people who had already crossed over. He didn't speak to dead people. I did. It was my path, my journey, not his. It is also part of my greatness—the ability to connect to the other side for others. Just because I do it doesn't mean he has to believe it or do the same. He brought something else to the table—the willingness and knowledge to help me get some much-needed "*zzzs*." Because of our diversity, he was able to help me. I sincerely appreciate my successes and know that I'm moving in the right direction toward realizing my vision of greatness.

• •

WEEK 36 EXERCISE:

WHAT YOU SEE IS WHAT YOU GET

The first few days, pull up from your internal Rolodex people who you've crossed paths with. Make note of how they've affected your life. Has it been positive? Has it been negative?

What did you learn from them? What did you teach them? Given the choice, would you do it all again?

Over the rest of the week, carry your journal with you. Write down the name of anyone you feel is trying to crush your vision. Record why you think they are. Include what they are doing (in your opinion) to sabotage your greatness. Also write down the names of others who seem to be encouraging or supporting you on your path, or even others on their own personal journey.

Manifesting

"What I think is what I see is what I am."

Chapter 8

The Act of Manifesting Greatness

(WEEKS 37–41)

Now for the How

Manifesting, again, is the act of creating or bringing into your life something that you do not yet possess. When you look at it in this way, it's quite easy to understand. However, that doesn't always mean you instinctively know how to manifest. It also doesn't mean you know exactly what the process should be to bring about your manifestations.

This chapter is dedicated to understanding the process you can use to guide you in opening up. There are five easy-to-follow steps, presented in a very direct yet incredibly enlightening approach. Enjoy each step, as that will indeed add to your overall goals outcome. This method is not intended to be a secret. By all means, share it with others—shout it from the rooftops! The more we all tap into this greatness that is so important to each and every one of us, the more our souls will be free to soar!

Learning how to manifest introduces you to the potential you have within you for greatness, as well as the endless possibilities that are available in every aspect of your life. Using everything you've learned about intuition will help you understand the energy that is ever-present—your gut instincts will kick in and assist you in pulling your greatness to the surface.

Step One: Your Light

Everybody has a light

We have a light within us. This light needs to be recognized and nourished. Some call it our potential; some call it our worth. When we believe in this light, our power grows, but ignoring it causes it to dim. The more we disregard our light, the more chance there is of it going out altogether, and we lose all sense of our significance.

This light may have been ignored or even forgotten about. It's easy to disregard it. After all, life happens. We work hard but seem to get nowhere, at least not anywhere we want to be. Doubt starts to creep in, causing us to question our desires, our worth, and our intentions. In turn, this creates a lack of self-esteem in many areas, a deficiency in health, and even an overall feeling of boredom.

We get stuck in the past, no longer looking forward to our future and unable to exist fully in the present. We've all got a past. Living in the past is what prevents us from living in our present. Get rid of what no longer works for you by letting go of what you don't need. You've gained an abundance of knowledge from all of the events in your past—both good and bad. That wisdom will always be there; it's the blows you took that let the light go out that you need to release yourself from. Then, and only then, will you find the radiance again.

Reigniting the light

We need to reignite the light you have inside you. It's been there all along—it was just blown out. In order to ignite that flame, you have to believe in its existence. A young client of mine, Carter, had a difficult time recognizing his spark until we addressed the direction his life had taken up to that point in time.

"I have no idea what's going on. Like, I can't stop thinking about everything at the same time, and I get so frustrated by everything and I overexaggerate what everyone says or does, even myself. It confuses me, and I can't figure out what to do," Carter told me one day.

Now, sometimes people just want me to tune in to their future; they don't want to deal with their past. Others are looking for sugarcoated answers so they can stay where they are and not have to think about it. I could tell that Carter really needed the truth.

"Want my honest, no-holds-barred read on that?"

"Yes, please. I need it!" he replied, happy, I think, that someone would be able to help him.

"Okay, here goes. You've learned to act out because you are frustrated that you don't get attention unless it's negative attention. This is something you've created. You are maturing now, so that doesn't feel right anymore. It's confusing, frustrating, and it's hard on your self-esteem. You beat yourself up and are always trying to figure out what went wrong. You've also learned to be a wiseass, and that's not working for you anymore either. You are a good kid. You have a need to be heard and have your opinions, thoughts, and ideas validated. When people don't do that for you, it's hard for you to give your loyalty, trust, and even acknowledgment back to them, so the whole cycle of frustration starts over again. You say things or do things you don't really want to do or you don't mean because you are used to utilizing this as your defense mechanism," I told him. I put it all on the table, knowing full well that Carter was feeling upset in the present because of what he had felt in the past.

"Okay, wow! That was scarily accurate," he concurred. "All right! I am going to process this and work on it."

"One step at a time, Carter. Letting go of the past, especially when it's how you've learned to live, can take time. And remember: people have also learned to react to you based on how they know you normally act. It will take time and effort for them to change their reaction to you as well." I continued. "Your light has only temporarily been extinguished. You can revive it."

"Okay. Thank you! Like, thank you a lot!" Carter replied, and I could feel the gears turning as he was rewinding and letting go. He was tuning in to what his intuition had been nudging him to understand. He recognized he had loving family and friends all around him and understood that he no longer needed the negative attention and would start trying to attract healthy attention through his own actions. By releasing what had previously worked for him, he would be able to make the changes necessary to move forward in a positive way. He needed to make the space in his life.

Our light not only needs to be nurtured, but it also needs to be uncovered in order to flourish. Just as a candle flame needs oxygen to burn, your magnificent light needs freedom to shine. By shedding the clutter and opening the space within your spirit, you will allow the light to ignite so you can move toward manifesting greatness. Jiddu Krishnamurti, the mystic and philosopher, said, "Without freedom from the past, there is no freedom at all." He was right. The past can hold us hostage, kept away from the light.

· ·

WEEK 37 EXERCISE:
THE LIGHT

A major step in manifesting greatness needs to be reigniting the light within you that coaxes that greatness up to the surface. Today, and over the next five days, begin by letting go of past events that no longer need to be acknowledged. Yes, you will retain the knowledge and wisdom from your past, but you don't need to wear it as a protective cover any longer.

Write down in your journal any events as far back as childhood when you were humiliated, embarrassed, harassed, teased, picked on, or bullied. Be honest with yourself. You may find there were many times when you've held on to mean and unsolicited opinions and criticisms—possibly because they came at a critical time in your life, or because you thought by holding on to them you'd grow from them, or even because you let yourself believe you may have deserved them in some way.

It's time to let them go. Go over each one and allow yourself a good cry. Get angry, punch a pillow. Let it out and let it go. It took a lifetime to create your past; it's going to take at least these few days to let it go.

On the sixth day, you are going to work on reigniting your light. You've let go of the blockages from the past. You are ready to move forward. Get a tall taper candle and some matches and go somewhere you can be comfortable for at least an hour, preferably longer.

Settle in and place the candle (in a holder) about a foot in front of you, unlit. Close your eyes and take a deep breath. Imagine your body becoming more and more relaxed. Imagine a beautiful pink and gold energy traveling through your body, beginning at the top of your head, going down through your neck and chest and arms and fingers. Allow that energy to warm you inside and out down through your abdomen, your hips, your thighs, your knees, your calves, your feet, and out through your toes. Let the energy swirl down your back and your spine. As it flows through you, it pushes out any residual energy from your past.

Now, take the matches and light the candle. Focus on the flame; watch it as it burns. Notice how the color changes and how the flame dances. Look at how big the flame is and how it grows and changes. Do you see anything in the flame? What images do you see? Continue watching it as the candle burns down. Pay special attention to how your body feels as you become one with the flame. Keep with it until you no longer feel a pull or connection to it.

On the seventh day, repeat the meditation. This time, though, instead of taking the matches and lighting an external candle, imagine that flame—the way it felt to you, the way it looked, and how it changed. Call up the images you saw or felt with the candle flame. Now imagine lighting that flame inside you. Feel your solar plexus area, and imagine the flame sparking and growing inside you. Visualize it; this is your light. Let it develop and travel up through your chest, your throat, and all the way up through your third eye and your head. Feel the warmth of your light as it spreads, growing bigger and bigger. Envision your flame expanding and swelling until the brightness begins shooting out of your body, your fingertips, and your toes.

This is your radiance! Let it shine! You've just reignited your light and begun manifesting your greatness!

Manifesting
"I am the light I wish to be in the world!"

. . . .

Step Two: Request

The act of requesting something means you are asking for something to be given to you or something to happen because you desire it. Requesting is about seeking or demanding something because you want it. Most importantly, right now, this is step two in manifesting greatness!

Just ask

I was doing a radio show recently. People called and wrote in with questions, hoping for psychic readings. Amy asked the question, "How can I get my angels to come to me in my dreams? I always want them to, but they never do. Is there something special I'm not doing?"

"Have you tried asking?" I answered simply.

"Really?" she said.

"Really," I repeated.

"Okay, you're kidding, right? There's got to be some secret you use to get your angels or guides to come in. Do you just not want to tell me?" she continued.

"No, I'm serious! Just ask them to come. When you put your request out into the universe, they can hear you. Your angels and guides and even deceased loved ones generally won't show up to help you unless you ask for it," I told her.

"Wow. I never thought of that. Just ask. What an idea!" she concluded.

Does your energy resonate with your desires?

She was right; it is an incredible concept and one that is crucial in the manifestation process. We need to express what we want and send it out to the universe. We also need to bring ourselves into a place of vibration where our energy resonates with what we want. Just because you ask for it doesn't mean you will get it; it has to work with who you are and what makes sense. For instance, if you have never wanted to go skiing before, or don't like to ski, chances are that asking to win the Olympic gold in the giant slalom is not going to happen. But possibly if you are already working hard and training and have a natural aptitude for it, you may make the official team. When you start this second step, you will only succeed if what you request is in alignment with your energy.

Your request has to be logical. What you're asking the world to provide has to be well-thought-out and detailed. While thoughts influence our life's path and what we magnetically draw into our life, these same thoughts can also assist the request we send out to the universe. You are bolstering and reinforcing what you are asking for, so the clearer you put forth your desires, the better your chances are of receiving them.

Alligator bag or live alligator?

My client Melissa came in looking for help with her career. She is a Reiki practitioner and was concerned because her practice was not growing as quickly as she'd hoped. She couldn't afford to advertise, so she was hoping to get some help with manifesting.

"I don't understand why it's not happening. I'm putting my intentions out there, and all I'm getting are phone calls, emails, and questions about what I do. Is it me? Do people not like me? Am I scary in some way? What's going on? I need to make money doing this or I'll have to stop. What can I do?" she asked, and I could tell she was almost at the end of her rope.

"I'm feeling like your requests to the universe do not quite match up with what you're actually hoping to achieve. You said you are working on your manifestations. What specifically are you asking for?" I questioned her.

"Well, I've been really good about saying every night and every morning, 'Please send people to me who are interested in what I do and want to know more about it.' I'm starting not to believe in manifesting anymore," she replied with a sad face.

"Aha! There it is. That's what's wrong!" I told her, excited because I'd just figured out the answer.

"What? What's it?"

"You are asking for interest in your business and what you do. You're getting that! You said a lot of people have contacted you. It's time for you to take the next step. You have to request more actual paying clients!" I said. I knew this was the answer.

"Oh, my goodness! I never thought about it that way! I absolutely will give it one last try. I hope this works!" she answered with enthusiasm.

"If it's for your greater good, it will. Be open to receiving and let me know what happens!"

Melissa contacted me a couple months later. Her business was picking up, and she'd doubled her actual paying clients. Being more specific had brought in what she was asking for. Don't be afraid to open the dialogue by stating exactly what it is you are requesting. Alignment with your wishes is part of your destiny. Knowing how to ask for it is part of your learning experience. Imagine loving alligator bags or shoes and asking the universe for more alligators. Wouldn't you rather have the UPS driver bring a bag to your door than have a live gator swimming in your pool? Think about it.

• •

WEEK 38 EXERCISE:

ASK FOR IT ALL

This week is all about carefully constructing your wants and desires so they can reach out into the ether to be fulfilled by the universe. On the first day, write down exactly what it is you think you want. Include every adjective you can to describe it. Spend some time with this. It's really important.

On the second day, do it again. Without looking at what you wrote on the first day, write what you are requesting from the universe. Remember, you are working on manifesting greatness, not just asking for chocolate ice cream. Record everything that can help you illustrate what you're hoping to achieve or receive. Be precise!

On the third day, do it again.

The fourth and fifth days, pull all of the descriptions together into one place. Do they match up? Eliminate what doesn't feel right or doesn't add to your explanation of what you are requesting. Once again, precision is crucial.

The next day, write it out on a single piece of paper: "For my greater good, I want _____, and I'd like to welcome it into my life by _____."

On the final day this week, bring your pen and paper with you and go somewhere in nature, a place that feels good and comfortable to you. Sit down on the earth, on a rock, or even in a stream. Take a deep breath and close your eyes, face toward the sun. Stay in this place until everything else melts away. Allow the energy to shine down upon you, filling you with warmth and love. Feel the sun's radiance travel down through your body and out the tips of your toes. When you're ready, take out your paper. Read it out loud, expressing your request to the universe, to God, your higher power. State it clearly and, as you do, visualize what it looks like, feel what it would feel like, smell its scent, and fill your request with your own wisdom and love.

Manifesting

**"I send out requests that will be fulfilled
to help me achieve my greatness."**

☺

Step Three: Acceptance

You have to accept that what you are manifesting can and will happen. We have been conditioned to mistakenly believe we may not be worthy of accepting gifts from the universe or that we can't possibly make anything happen by sheer will or spiritual belief alone. That is a mistake. We live in a demanding world—one that challenges us to work as hard as we possibly can to make money to pay for the things we want, or think we need, so we can spend time with our families. The problem is, because of the desire for money, we're always working, so we don't have the opportunity to spend those moments together. By now, we have to imagine there is a better way to become one with our spirit and the universe.

We are one

Now, I'm going to let you in on a secret. This may be one of the most influential or even controversial ideas you've ever heard, so … hold on. God, the universal energy of love, is around us all the time—spreading through us, swirling, and connecting everyone. We are made of this energy, part of this energy, and everlasting. Our spirits or our souls are one; our energy is vast and intertwined and the same all at once. This is what makes psychic and intuitive abilities possible. Our grand energy keeps our deceased loved ones, angels, and guides accessible to us. Accepting that your request will be heard and can be provided for is easier now, isn't it?

Wayne Dyer states, "Manifesting is not about getting things that are not here. It is about attracting what is already here and is part of you on a spiritual level." But it doesn't mean what you are hoping to manifest will just show up on your doorstep, wrapped in a pretty red bow when you go outside in the morning. You have to make space to allow the changes to happen. For instance, if your greatness involves traveling the world and speaking to large audiences fifty different times this year, then planning to have a baby at the same time would be counterproductive. Instead, cut back on your activities; give yourself a little wiggle room. By creating the space in your busy life, you are telling the universe you are ready for the gifts you wish to receive. The good news is you've already begun this process. By letting go of the past, you have opened up and can allow new blessings and opportunities that are in alignment with your spirit to appear.

Participate in your life

It's not quite enough to sit back and wait to be bestowed with greatness. You have to be an active participant in your own life. Recognize opportunities that are put in your path to greatness and utilize them. If you are looking to manifest wealth, you wouldn't step over a five-dollar bill without picking it up off the floor, would you? Manifesting greatness is the same thing. If you are hoping to eradicate cancer, don't turn down a job at the foremost research lab that's looking for a cure.

Trust that your request is being heard and will be answered. Accept that you are able to attract what you wish because you are already connected to all the energy in the universe. Know that regardless of who you are, everyone has dreams of greatness. Marilyn Monroe said, "Beneath the makeup and behind the smile, I am just a girl who wishes for the world." Accepting that you are worthy and manifestation is real can attract you to greatness that will change your entire being. Be ready for it!

• •

WEEK 39 EXERCISE:

ACCEPT IT

During this week, you need to accept that you can and will manifest greatness. Let go of any doubts you may have. Every day, think about what you are requesting of the universe. Any time you feel any negativity or doubt creeping in, send it away. Breathe deeply and allow it to fade and fall back into the earth. Focus on your light and allow it to expand inside you, filling you with love and greatness.

Manifesting

"I accept that _____will be manifested and that I am already part of the energy."

✍ ☺

• •

Step Four: Have Faith

The fourth step in manifesting greatness may very well be the hardest. Having faith is difficult. Faith is about believing in something even though you have no evidence to prove its truth. Faith is having trust in, or being confident in, something when there's no logical reason to. Faith is believing, though your brain tells you not to. Faith is an extension of your heart's energy toward something intangible.

No control

You've already learned in step three to accept that the energy of manifestation is real and that you are deserving of the gifts it brings. Step four is about letting go of controlling how the offerings are brought about. At this point you need to step away from the actual process of calculating how getting what you want will happen. You need to have faith that God or the universe will create what you need, deliberately, so it works specifically for you. This is different from what most of us are used to. Normally, we direct our energy; having faith means letting the universe direct it for us.

Ben has been a cabinetmaker for over twenty-five years. For the first fifteen, he worked for other people. He got married, bought a house, and had a baby. All the while, he dreamt of starting his own business. His wife, Stephanie, kept telling him she agreed, but that it wasn't the right time. Stephanie is intuitive. She knew it would happen but was concerned about making so many changes in such a short time frame. The universe, however, had quite a different idea about it.

They had both been putting it out into the ether that they wanted Ben to start his own business, but there had to be enough money to make it worth it and have it work out. To give up a steady paycheck and a good job was craziness when they had just taken on a big mortgage and had a child.

They lived from paycheck to paycheck for a year after the baby was born. Ben's potential was stifled by the need to be responsible and pay the bills, as he felt it wouldn't be safe financially to begin his own business. Even though the security of the job made them confident they could meet their expenses, they weren't content, feeling there was no moving up for him and she'd be stuck in a career she wasn't happy with. Then, the universe stepped up. The intention and thoughts of the couple had manifested and they were provided with an opportunity. A contractor offered him a big job, but Ben had to commit to working on it full time. It was the chance they had been waiting for. Fifteen years later, he's still on his own, with his own shop and clientele. He's never had to advertise, though there have been some financially shaky times for them over the years. They were so busy living and figuring out their day-to-day lives that they didn't try and control how their requests to the universe were fulfilled.

Barbara Mark and Trudy Griswold write in their book *Angelspeake*, "There will be a temptation to meddle. Letting it happen is the hardest part." Your desire to manifest greatness is significant in your journey. To fully accept and appreciate that this desire can be realized, you need that faith.

• •

WEEK 40 EXERCISE:
YOU GOTTA HAVE FAITH

Faith that you will be aligned with your path is all you need this week. Over the first few days, get out your journal and record what you have faith in. Do you believe in a higher power?

Do you have faith that things happen for a reason? Do you put your faith in something unknown? Do you have faith that you will be gifted with whatever you need? Write it all down.

The rest of the week, believe that God and the universe will provide you with what you requested. Your manifestation can continue without your need to control the particulars. So, enjoy your freedom this week and don't even think about having to be in charge of any of the details. You have a life to continue living; have faith that all will be provided!

Manifesting

"I have faith the universe will provide without my control."

Step Five: Appreciate

We may love what we have. Are we always thankful for it? When I do readings for my clients, I do a meditation to call in my deceased loved ones, my guides, and angels to help. I also ask my clients' deceased loved ones to come through with messages my clients will understand. After my session I thank the universe for helping me to understand the communications I've shared with the client. I feel like I need to express my gratitude for letting me give back to others with my gifts. Gratitude conveys our appreciation back to the universe.

The universe is generous

We are grateful for the birds in the sky. We're thankful for the trees, and newborn babies and puppies and love. Saying thank you is all that's expected from the universe. When we receive something, we show our appreciation. Our thanks provides closure. It helps complete the circle and leaves us open to the next gift. The universe is generous. The more gratitude we share, the more abundant our lives become.

A "lack of" can cause a feeling of being passed over or ignored. This can create anger or frustration and can destroy our confidence in achieving or receiving anything. When we are like this, we stay stuck in a place of scarcity because we don't feel worthy or deserving of having more. Believing you don't have and won't have attracts more "lack of." Instead, appreciate everything. Have an attitude of gratitude. Enjoy the precious little moments and the people and, yes, the stuff that you have. Stop living in scarcity.

In step five, it's time to express your appreciation to the universe for your anticipated manifestation of greatness. The only thing at this point that can hold you back is your attitude. Being thankful and communicating your aspiration for greatness can help push your wants and desires further into the ether. No one else can make you give thanks. It's something we feel from within. We need to cultivate it and develop our gratitude so it becomes a natural, everyday occurrence. Appreciate what the universe is going to provide for you.

Appreciate

I am lucky. I am blessed. I am thankful for my children and my husband and my friends and my family and everything I have in my life. I am humbled that I have so many clients that leave my office expressing their absolute gratitude for the readings I've given them. Often, I've given hope or closure. Connecting them to their deceased loved ones allows them to feel like they haven't totally lost them. For this, they are filled with appreciation. "I just had to thank you for today! I was blown away by what you had to say!" is a typical email from a new client. It is this that I appreciate, this I give thanks for: the opportunity I have to share my gift, as well as the chance to teach others to share their gratitude.

The last step in manifesting your greatness is merely giving thanks to the universe for what it's giving you—now and always.

• •

WEEK 41 EXERCISE:

THANK YOU

For those who are used to appreciating who they are and what they have, this week will be easy. For others, who complain often or feel angry that they don't have enough, it may be a bit more difficult.

Thank the universe for everything you are. Look toward the sky and spin around and spread your arms out wide, spreading your gratitude to the world. Express your appreciation specifically for the anticipated gift of manifesting greatness.

Every day afterward, for the entire week, upon waking and right before sleep, say, "Thank you." Go further. Say thank you all day long: to the dry cleaner and to the drive-thru employee at the coffee shop, to the educator who teaches your son, the coach who coaches your daughter, the spouse who said you were beautiful, and even to the car in front of you that is driving 10 mph in a 30 mph zone. Appreciate everyone and everything this week. You'll find you are much happier, more content, and more at peace with your life.

Manifesting

"I am thankful every day for _____."

✍ ☺

• •

. . . .

Chapter 9

Living the Dream

(WEEKS 42–52)

A New You

You are smart. You are intuitive. You are generous. You are kind. And you are reinventing yourself by simply reading this book. It was a concentrated effort to make the changes necessary to begin your search for your internal greatness. That was the beginning. You are well on your way and are capable of achieving what you want. C. S. Lewis said, "You are never too old to set another goal or to dream a new dream." He was right.

No content

By doing the exercises in this book, you have created a new and intuitive you, a changed version of the old person. You have opened yourself up to the reality that there is more to life than what you've previously experienced. You've also glimpsed both physically and intuitively, at least in some small way, a world that may have been layers upon layers within yourself. The work that you've done and all of the goals you've achieved and everything you've attained thus far make up what your life has been all about.

Greatness—the inner greatness, the brilliance that is your true spirit—is not about the content that you fill your life with. It is, instead, who you truly are. Your aura is spreading out and expanding. In his book *A New Earth*, Eckhart Tolle writes, "Most people define themselves through the content of their lives…Content is what absorbs most people's attention entirely, and it is what they identify with." By tuning in to your spirit and working the exercises and manifestings within these pages, you've not only tapped into your essence but you've also begun feeling your greatness.

You are not only your external shell; you are also your spirit, your soul, your greatness. Are you ready to show that to the world? We cover up and protect our spirit so as not to be exposed. Our lives are protected by our stuff—what we share with everyone. Our hopes and dreams, our goals, get us closer to the energy we truly are. You are now at an important fork in the road. Manifesting more content in your life is perfectly acceptable—as a matter of fact, it's probably preferable. To give up that content and reveal your true spirit is more than difficult; it's almost impossible. The key, however, is becoming connected to that fundamental core, the essence of who you are. You've opened that pathway and are on your journey to understanding the person you can be.

Law of attraction

While manifesting, you are giving yourself access to abundance in every respect. How much you receive is inherently and energetically up to you. In this refreshed version of you, magnetizing that which is positive is crucial. Attracting what will help propel you to become a better person will contribute to raising your energy. This, then, will increase your abundance as well.

You are one of a kind, and the fact that you are sharing your energy with others, even more than before, will help attract and manifest positive energy back to yourself. According to Rhonda Byrne,

"The law of attraction is a sticky business. When you rejoice in another person's good fortune, their good fortune sticks to you!" You have begun creating a new you, a new life. Your appreciation and respect for others will karmically be returned to you.

You have manifested so much so far, in only a short time. There is no reason to cut that short. Friends will also reap the benefits of your new life. Your improved outlook and energy will spread out like ripples on a pond. Think of the butterfly effect. When the wings of a butterfly flap, the energy is sent out to the universe and transforms everything in its path. You are not powerless; your reach stretches beyond what your imagination can fathom. The universe wants you to continue improving and expanding your life. It's your world and it doesn't just happen to you. Listen to your intuitive voice. You get to direct it and make it an incredible one.

- -

WEEK 42 EXERCISE:
YOUR NEW LIFE

You've come a long way. Take the first five days and go over everything you've done so far while doing the exercises and opening up to your intuition. Review everything you've entered in your journal. You might be amazed at how much you've accomplished!

During the rest of the week, write down what stands out the most to you about your new way of looking at your world. What do you resonate with? What doesn't feel right? What's your favorite part about everything you've accomplished? Record all of your thoughts. Remember, you have just begun!

Manifesting

"Every day, in every way, I am getting better and better."

- -

Building the Dream

Your attitude determines your altitude; you'll only go as far as you allow yourself to believe. You need to believe in yourself to achieve your dreams. When you see a vision of your future, what does it look like? Does it involve happiness? Sadness? Wealth? Poverty? Pride? Shame? Do you see, in your mind's eye, friends around you sharing in an abundant life? Or are you alone, a single person navigating a solemn world? What you believe, you can achieve.

Your dreams matter

Your reality now is based on what you develop and what you manifest. Your authenticity need not be challenged, because your ideas are your own. Intuition has shown you what your environment can be, and your dreams have taught you what's possible. It's about more than just money or power, as you've learned throughout the stories and exercises in this book. These things can be part of your reality, but they are not the be-all and end-all. Your hopes are based on your reality and what you want—not what anyone else wants. And you matter. Your dreams matter.

Engaging your community, friends, and family in your life are a critical part of building your dreams. Being involved enables you to learn, and that in turn helps create a desire. Where there is a desire, there is bound to be a dream of making something better or increasing your abundance. Dreams don't stop because you've made one a reality. They continue and even multiply when you realize how much more there is to shoot for.

Having your friends around you to support you as you shoot for your dreams will add to your ability to see outside your own personal arena and gives you someone to share your hopes with. Building a dream involves constructing a change in your life. Making it a joyful life is easier with people you care about. Your hopes and dreams are amplified.

Expansion

December 12, 2012, was touted as a day of expansion. I had many people who contacted me to ask what this meant.

"Expansion? Does that mean I'm going to gain weight?" one person asked me.

"No," I told them. "This date, 12/12/12, is a day of expansion, which suggests you can expand or make your place in the world bigger. You have an exaggerated chance to increase your worth, your value."

"Why? Can't we do that every day? I thought when we manifested we could do anything?"

That gave me something to really think about. I pondered what it could possibly mean. To suggest that we could expand our spiritual footprint every day was a great idea to share. I knew it already but never looked at it so precisely before. It made me realize that teaching others to continue to build their dreams would increase their abundance. We didn't to have a specific date to enlarge their energy. At the same time, however, I realized that days like that—specifically one that will never happen again in this lifetime—should be looked at as a reminder or a wake-up call to awaken your greatness and follow your destiny.

The mountain

When I imagine goals in my mind's eye, I always see a mountain or a hill. At the top of the mountain is the achievement of my goal. Using your intuitive awareness, you can envision the hill and see that along the path leading upward there are crevices that you can fall into, and rocks and dirt that can cause you to slip backward. There are also flowers at random locations on the way up. Those crevices and sliding earth represent the setbacks you will stumble upon on your way to achieving those goals. The flowers are the blooming potential and growth and even some smaller dreams being realized as you go.

Those blossoms are your potential and the feedback you need to encourage you to continue building your dream.

When you create an image or a personal symbol, it allows you to measure or gauge your progress. In this way it gives you smaller goals you can celebrate along the steady way to greatness!

. . . .

WEEK 43 EXERCISE:
BELIEVING THE DREAM

On the first day, write down what dreams you've worked on so far using the exercises in the book. Which have come true? Which are still brewing? Write them down in two different columns. Then note what has happened around them, or what has come to fruition. For example, if you wanted an increase in money, did you get it? How much? Write this information down.

On the second day, meditate, choosing one of the previous exercises that has felt good to you, positive for you, or that you've connected with, and take some time to visualize what your journey looks like. As I shared before, my visualization of my journey toward my goal is a mountain. Yours can also be a mountain, but it doesn't have to be. Imagine it, everything about it, what it looks like, feels like, smells like. This, then, can be used for other goals or just for a dream you have today.

You've got greatness bubbling inside you. Who's along for the ride? During the next few days, tune in to your intuition and look at who is still in your life during the building of your dreams, as well as who is still there when you reach the top of your mountain.

On the fifth or six day, check your intuitive vision and look at what blossoms are on the hill or your version of the hill. What are you expanding on?

On the final day or two, record dreams and goals you still have. What are you still hoping for? What are you wishing for? Make a list of goals you may or may not yet be working on. Do you believe they can become reality? Do you feel you can reach the top with them? As you focus on each one, feel how your chakras relate to them. Do you feel a stir anywhere? Write down the dreams and goals that felt good. It's time to put them out into the universe.

Manifesting

"I feel the mountain on my way up and recover easily, learning from every pitfall."

Sharing the Dream

You have your own point of view, your own desires, and your own dreams. You've gotten this far by yourself; no one else has done it for you. This is an incredible feat on its own, but coupled with the fact that you are now stepping into your power, it's amazing. You are awakening to your purpose. By continuing your individuality, you've earned an even larger place in the universe. You are gaining momentum. Staying true to your energy, intuition, and spirit is very important.

Give and take

Sharing your energy with others is a wonderful way to expand your energy as well. We all like to share our lives with others, and as you read earlier in this chapter, doing so helps elevate your energy. By teaching others what you've learned, you enhance your knowledge as well. The best way to learn is to share what you know. It validates your significance and your contribution. Learning from others, and sharing their energy, also increases your energy and your wisdom.

Author Anthony Douglas Williams said, "Knowledge comes from learning. Wisdom comes from living."

When you share, it shows how much you care about someone else and their well-being. As with the law of attraction, what you give out you receive back. When you share your spirit with others, you can be pretty sure that what you will get in return will be even greater. Being greedy with your possessions, who you are, and what you've manifested will only bring you heartache in return. Manifesting means you leave your ego behind. This leaves you wide open, so you have space to include others in your greatness.

Universal energy unites

There is a limit to your sharing, however. You are your own person, and you cannot intentionally manifest something in your life if it's not for your own good or the betterment of you. This is not to say that you can't or don't create negative manifestations when you put out negative energy. However, when you try and bring something into your life through manifestation that isn't in alignment with you or your needs or desires, it will not work. It may even make you feel sick. You simply can't manifest anything just because someone else wants you to.

In the grand scheme of things, we all share in a universal energy that unites us. Therefore, the energy of the requests and desires someone else wants spreads to every one of us. This is one of the reasons it's so incredibly important to think positively, to let go of all thoughts of scarcity or lack, and instead focus on love. Love, truly, is all you need.

· ·

WEEK 44 EXERCISE:

SHARING

Over the first few days of this week, you need to get out that journal. Write down times you've shared your energy with someone. This will take quite a while because you need to go all the way back to childhood. Record any specific instances that stand out to you and also write about how you remember each instance feeling.

Over the next few days, write down instances when you've tried to manifest something only because someone else wanted you to. For example, your wife wants you to manifest a change in your job to include no more travel even though you were fine with it. Or, your husband wants you to work on manifesting a bigger home, but you like yours the way it is. Essentially, this is change you are trying to bring about for someone because they want it, not because you want it. How did it feel? Did it work for you? What was the outcome?

During the final days of the week, go out and share your energy with someone! Work on learning from and teaching someone else. Do you feel their energy? Does it feel good to share?

Manifesting

Today, share your knowledge of manifestation with someone. Remember, we are all part of the universal energy and we share the benefits.

Feeling the Power

Powerful beyond belief, you have strength that is immeasurable. You don't need to bend to someone else's will or ignore other people. When focused, you are on. Your energy is incredible. But when you tap into the energy of manifesting greatness using your intuition, you are on fire.

The power of salmon

Sometimes it's hard to recognize how incredibly powerful you are. Take a look at salmon. That's right, the fish. At first glance, they are not powerful. They are a simple fish—one that we eat. But think about how they survive. They are born in a river, travel out to the ocean, and then swim back, all the way back, to fight their way upstream to spawn and begin the cycle again. Now, maybe you think that's crazy. The cycle never changes, never ends. But think about their focus, their power that drives them to have the strength and the wherewithal to make that trek. They are powerful. You, also, may not recognize your power.

Powerful accomplishments

Give yourself a moment to ponder everything you've accomplished since you first picked up this book. You've identified your idea of success and recognized successful people. You've opened up and discovered your intuitive abilities, those same abilities that help you look to your future, recognize synchronicities, feel energy, and tune in to the other side. You have worked on manifesting for almost a year and you've discovered who you are through your core values. Symbols have become part of your life, and you've sent out your request to manifest your own personal greatness to the universe. Now, again, imagine the power you possess. It's incredible.

You are an amazing being, loaded with fruitful responsibilities and chores, but amazing nonetheless. Being human does not limit your power; rather, it increases it. This limitless power needs to be utilized, experienced, and unleashed so that the greatness you are discovering within you can transcend from your human boundaries to your soul. We are indeed residing in a physical body, spiritual beings at the core. When we tap into the power that is within us, our light will glow stronger than we can imagine.

Power for power's sake

Awakening and employing our power does not imply in any way that we need to take power or confidence away from anyone else. This power that you are coming into, and recognizing as yours, does not come from anywhere but within yourself—the universal energy that swirls through you. Hijacking someone else's self-esteem or confidence for the benefit of yours does not count as, but rather takes away from, your own power.

Your power is waiting to break free. It is slowly coming out but is still bound by self-imposed barriers. We are afraid to let it glow because of the changes it would make in our lives. You are aware of this greatness now. To ignore it and not use it from this point forward would be like giving away your right to assert your free will. It would be an exercise in futility. Now that you recognize your power, you have no option but to pursue your goals. This said, it will absolutely change your life. You have the power to make it better!

· ·

WEEK 45 EXERCISE:
POWERFUL

Occasionally, we feel like we have no power or that our power has been usurped by someone else. On the first day, write down any times in your life that stand out as significant, when you felt your power was taken away or that you had to shelf your power because someone else had more authority over you. Be precise in how you describe these instances. What do you think was done to you or against you? What was squashed? Who do you feel did it? Do you feel you let them? Or do you feel you had no choice?

On the second day, record how each event felt. Did you feel powerless? Did you experience a loss of confidence? What were your emotions around each event?

On the third day, record a time or times you felt you took someone else's power away from them. Did you do it intentionally? Did you regret it? Do you felt they deserved it? Would you do it again?

The next day, apologize. If you took someone's power from them intentionally and have regrets, make amends to them. If this is not possible to do in person, imagine you are telling them by writing an apology letter that you can either send or not send; it's entirely up to you. By telling them you're sorry, you are admitting you were wrong or inconsiderate, but you're also sending that positive energy into the universe.

For the rest of the week, tune in to your power. Does it make you feel like you can accomplish more? Do you feel like your confidence has increased? Is it easier to disregard when others try and usurp your power?

Manifesting

"I am powerful beyond belief."

☺

Summing It Up

It is truly remarkable how much you have grown while reading this book and doing the exercises and manifestations. You and those around you will never be the same. Whether you'd already begun your quest for greatness or you just started when you picked up this book doesn't matter. You've changed for the better.

A success

Success, as defined earlier, is about reaching the pinnacle of worthiness. To some, a plethora of money can be involved, but is not necessarily the meaning of success. For most, success is more about becoming someone others look up to and admire because you are a good person. It is about being at one with who you are and what you do. Success represents loving yourself and being in alignment with who you are in your career, spiritually, and emotionally. Success is a cornucopia of glee.

You've come to understand that your idea of success can and will change over time. However, there will be a common theme. It is important to love who you are and also to love your actions. You will never be successful if you neglect yourself. When you are acting in a way that doesn't feel right, or that hasn't come from a place of love, you've fallen off of your path. Your journey includes all of your successes as well as your mistakes, but your path takes you to your greatness. Experiencing happiness with what you are doing and who you are lets you know you are back on course.

I see, I am, I know

Intuition plays a significant role in figuring out what direction to go in. Understanding the messages and the symbols you receive from the other side, from God, from your deceased family and friends, can help you clarify your direction. By tuning in to your sixth sense, you are opening your energy to an incredible source, drawing from the spirit of the universe, from God, your loved ones. As you learned, we are all connected, though different in time and space. No matter what you call it—intuition, energy, or even physics—we have the power to know everything and be everything. Tapping into this intuitive source will aid us in manifesting whatever we need or, more importantly, what's best for our soul in order to manifest greatness.

I saw the signs

Recognizing signs and synchronicities is another way we use our intuitive abilities to manifest greatness. Once we identify synchronistic events, it's hard to deny their existence or to write them off as mere coincidence. Just as we are all one, the signs and synchronicities we experience are connected and are there to help guide us and show us what to do next or where to go or who to be with. It's not about the events themselves, but rather it's the instructions they represent that are so important to us as we continue our journey.

Shocking, isn't it?

Becoming acquainted with the energy that we are made of and how to utilize it helps to put things in perspective. Our aura, the energy we project off of our body, can be altered or adapted when we direct our attention to it. By using our psychic awareness or scientifically using special electromagnetic measurements or Kirlian photography, which shows the electric coronal discharge, we are able to see how the size and shape of our own energy field can change and can even merge with someone else's. Recognizing the way our energy flows, when we are attempting something with someone specific, can help us distinguish how to best live contentedly—fulfilled and aware.

Our chakra system, or spiritual batteries, keeps us in check. It alerts us when we are out of balance or missing something in our lives. It can also show us when there is an overabundance causing anything from extreme fatigue to total confusion. When our chakras are aligned, we are at peace. When they aren't spinning properly, we experience discord and have a hard time moving from the current place we are in. Having all of our energy centers tuned in to each other and our spirit allows us to feel a sense of freedom and joy and can even help us to physically feel better and healthier.

The can can

Coming from a place of "I can" instead of "I can't" helps positive energy travel through you and around you. This positive energy is sent out to the universe and automatically attracts like or positive energy back to you. It's like a boomerang effect; what you send out, you get back. However, the same is true for negative energy. When you are constantly complaining or blaming others or sitting in judgment, the same energy will be returned. Essentially, you get what you give. That's why it is crucial to stay positive. Although this can be difficult at times, it becomes easier when everything you do stems from love rather than fear.

Moral compass

Staying positive also has to align with your core values. While truth and honesty are significant core values, so are playfulness and courage. No matter what your personal core values are, you will connect easier with your spirit and your ability to manifest in your life when you are living within these principles you have discovered and set for yourself. Morals play a key role in how you conduct your life; and when you are not in accordance with them, your energy is totally skewed. This can cause you to spin out of control and lose instead of gain momentum as your world crumbles. Your steps to manifesting will be disrupted, both internally and externally, and you'll find yourself steeped in drama.

Singing the blues

Respect for yourself and others will dwindle if your foundation is shaky, and you'll be singing the blues. On the other hand, tapping into your spiritual strength and your emotional and mental strengths can aid in earning respect again. Respecting who you are becomes less of a challenge when you stay true to your beliefs and your values. Kindness and gratitude go a long way toward creating a life you are proud of and respect. There is nothing more powerful than being in alignment with your true purpose—when you are, nothing will hold you back. You will manifest greatness because it's inside of you already, bubbling its way to the surface.

I see

Visualization helps to clarify wants and desires and also what we need more of or less of. Accessing the symbolic language assists in validating our connection with the universe and God and the energy that is transmitted within us and around us. Visualizing your future empowers you to look beyond your current situation and extend your reach into what you've already begun manifesting.

Manifesting brilliance

Your light is brilliant now, allowing you to request more from the universe. It's brighter because you accept the possibility that there is more to be accomplished and manifested. Your faith that you are part of a spectacular energy has brought you to a place of appreciation and gratitude for the anticipated goodies God is raining upon you. It is your time to shine, and you are ready to participate in the manifestation of your own greatness.

Like the salmon swimming upstream, you have come home to rejuvenate, to experience rebirth in all its splendor. Joy is prevalent because you are in a unique process of creation. There is no turning back and no one has the power to control you or take your greatness away from you. Everything you've accomplished is beginning to come to fruition; allow greatness to manifest!

. . . .

WEEK 46 EXERCISE:

RECHARGING

Spend this week recharging your spirit. It might be challenging, but you can do it. Look at all of the exercises you've done thus far. Is there anything you need to add to them or take away from them? Have you been totally honest with yourself? Have you included situations (where applicable) that you may be ashamed of or that were even mean-spirited? Have you written down things you've done or wanted that were maybe a bit embarrassing?

This week, recharge your spirit by going over every one of the exercises and making sure you haven't neglected any of them by being untrue to your spirit. If there is anything missing, fill it in now. Make the necessary changes. Allow the act of unloading any and all of your feelings, burdens, or unbalanced activities to fill you with love. Let the warmth of that energy spread. Your spirit, now, emanates good will toward everyone around you. Love it!

Manifesting

"I am ready!"

☺
. . . .

Go Forth and Prosper!

Reaching the summit

You've no doubt experienced ups and downs throughout the pages of this book. You've reached new highs and explored new lows. There have been exercises and manifestings that have resonated with you so you've enjoyed them. But there have also been some experiences that may have been difficult to face or deal with. Shedding old ways and making space for new ones can be rough, but you've maintained a desire, a need maybe, to continue pursuing what is necessary to reach the summit of who you can be. You are ready to take on the world.

Awareness has settled in, and you know you are primed to tap into the stream that belongs to you. In his book *Having It All*, John Assaraf said, "It's time to celebrate your inherent greatness and to understand you were created perfectly." It's already there, this magnificence that you are. Now is your chance to reclaim it and make it your own. You have this lifetime to understand what you're here to do and become, and it's never too late.

My greatness

I was happily married. I was the controller of a company. I thought it was awesome. I was young, in a great position, ready to take on the world. Until my world changed. My focus was redirected. I had a baby. The most unfathomable joy spread through me, and I knew it was the beginning of a new world. Then I had to return to work. I cried every day, having to leave my perfect baby girl, albeit in the arms of a loving grandmother. But I cried nonetheless. This new gift from the heavens showed me I was not where I was supposed to be. Early metaphysical leader and teacher Christian D. Larson said, "Believe in yourself and all that you are. Know that there is something inside you that is greater than any obstacle." I knew this had to be true.

I followed my intuition, which directed me to pursue something I had envisioned but not understood from many, many years prior to that moment of realization. I opened up a store, following my old vision of having a boutique. It was there that I was able to bring Molly, my precocious baby, and spend time with her, nurturing her and raising her to be a strong and loving young lady. A few years later, I had another incredible baby girl—Samantha. She was full of energy from the top of her crazy curls to the tips of her tiny toes. With Samantha came another shift in direction. What I had previously experienced—feeling like I was hit over the head and told, "You need to do this work now"—was coming to fruition. All my years of practice and rehearsing culminated into who I now am and who I'm still becoming.

Following my spirit has led me to be exactly where I need to be, so many times, in so many ways. I am still manifesting my greatness. I intuitively feel there is so much more to come and am excited and open to the vast possibilities. Every day I psychically see the next step, the bigger picture, and I know I am on my way there. Yet I am enjoying every minute of being where I am, in this moment, this second, right now. As I sit, typing, I am smiling.

If you can't imagine it, you can't manifest it. Start imagining your greatness! It will come, maybe a little at a time, but it will come. My heart aches, in a magnificent way, with the desire and knowledge that there is more out there for all of us. There is room to accomplish so much and to spread love, kindness, and joy to everyone.

When you can imagine it, you can manifest it. Open your imagination! You are on your way to manifesting greatness using your intuition!

• •

WEEK 47 EXERCISE:
IMAGINE!

The final exercises are all part of this chapter. Take your time and spread them out! In the long run, you'll be better off!

This week, imagine. Imagine different ways you can change your life. Imagine things that would make you happy. Write them down! Are you doing any of these things? Why or why not? Visualize what your life would look like if you were!

Manifesting
"I am changing for the better!"

WEEK 48 EXERCISE:
NOT HAPPENING?

This week is about exploring why some of your manifestations may not be happening yet.

- Is it for your greater good? If you are hoping to get something that doesn't resonate with who you are or where you need to be, you may not get it. Do you really want it?
- Do you believe in what you're asking for? Asking the universe to give you something when you don't believe it to be possible is setting yourself up for failure. You need to accept that it is possible!
- Have you set a deadline? Is it realistic? Setting an unrealistic deadline can cut off your gifts because it is not time for these things to be brought into your life. Not setting a deadline can leave it open to the universe to bring the gifts anytime into the future, instead of now, when you actually want them.
- Have you let go of the past? Holding on to things you no longer want in your life can sabotage your moving forward. Feeling that you are never going to get out of living in a personal world of "scarcity," for example, will hold you hostage there.
- Are you communicating your desires clearly? Are you asking for an orange when what you really want is an apple? Be specific!
- Are you recognizing opportunities as they come? Not being an active participant in your life will hinder the manifestation process. You don't need to control it, but you need to take the opportunities as they present themselves that will further you on your journey toward manifesting greatness!
- Do you believe you deserve more? If you are stuck with a subconscious or even conscious belief that you don't deserve more than what you have, you will not receive it. Change that belief! You are a spiritual being, worthy and deserving!

- Are you sending out positive vibes? If you are constantly criticizing or judging others, you are projecting negative energy. Remember, karma or the boomerang effect are in play here—what you give out, you get back!
- Are there other things you need to accomplish first? Sometimes we manifest in stages. You are not instantly going to become a famous psychic without putting any time into being an actual and legitimate psychic!

Manifesting

"This week I will change _____
to help my manifestation process."

WEEK 49 EXERCISE:
IMAGINE ONE YEAR FROM NOW

Relax somewhere that you won't be disturbed. Close your eyes and imagine a beautiful white and gold bubble of protection around you. See how sparkly it is, filled with positive energy. Imagine that it's somewhat opaque, difficult to see through and hazy enough to keep you safe.

Now imagine that inside this bubble you have a pair of magical binoculars that extend through the bubble's protective layer. On these special long-distance glasses there is a time setting that you can adjust.

Turn the dial to a date that is exactly 365 days from now and look through the binoculars at your future.

See where you are one year from now. Does it fit where you'd like to be? Do you look happy? Who's with you, if anyone? Have you manifested changes? Can you see what those manifestations have created for you? Have these changes made space in your life for more to come?

Take the time to really explore what you intuitively feel needs to be adjusted to make where you see yourself a year from now into a reality, if you don't already see it. Write it down. By writing it down, you are putting your intentions out into the universe!

Manifesting

"My accomplishments are incredible!"

WEEK 50 EXERCISE:
IMAGINE FIVE YEARS FROM NOW

Using the meditation of the bubble from the previous exercise, begin relaxing. Again, pick up the binoculars. This time, set the time dial for five years from now.

It's been a while! Does your life appear to have changed? Does it look different than it did at the one-year mark? What's different? What's the same? What were you hoping for? Did it happen? Again, write it down!

Manifesting

"I see the changes within me!"

WEEK 51 EXERCISE:
MANIFEST GREATNESS USING YOUR INTUITION

Congratulations! You've made it! This is your last week of work, but it's just the beginning! This final time should be spent going back and redoing any of the exercises in the book.

Pick the ones that challenged you the most. Are they any easier now? Pick also the ones you resonated with. Do they still feel good in your energy?

What the heck—do them all again! Enjoy the process!

Manifesting

"I Am Great!"

WEEK 52 EXERCISE:

RELAX

Get out all of the "write it down" affirmations you've put into your box and read them. Do they still feel good? Do they resonate with who you are now? You don't need to adjust them or make changes to them—just read and review what you've written. If you strongly feel you're guided to rewrite them, go ahead, but do it by crossing out and writing on the same paper. This way you can see how much you've grown during this year.

Relax! Do nothing else this week! You've worked hard! Take a break and just be.

This is your grand finale, but truly this is just the beginning!

Bibliography
and Suggested Reading

Alvarez, Melissa. *365 Ways to Raise Your Frequency: Simple Tools to Increase Your Spiritual Energy for Balance, Purpose, and Joy.* Woodbury, MN: Llewellyn Worldwide, 2012.

Andrews, Mark, Steve Purcell, Brenda Chapman, and Irene Mecchi. *Brave*, directed by Mark Andrews and Brenda Chapman (2012; Burbank, CA: Disney-Pixar, 2012), DVD.

Andrews, Ted. *The Healer's Manual: A Beginner's Guide to Energy Therapies.* St. Paul, MN: Llewellyn Worldwide, 2003.

Assaraf, John. *Having It All: Achieving Your Life's Goals and Dreams.* New York: Atria Books, 2003.

Barnum, Melanie. *The Book of Psychic Symbols: Interpreting Intuitive Messages.* Woodbury, MN: Llewellyn Worldwide, 2012.

Belanger, Michelle. *The Psychic Energy Codex: Awakening Your Subtle Senses.* San Francisco: Red Wheel/Weiser, LLC, 2007.

Brontë, Anne. *The Tenant of Wildfell Hall.* London: Smith, Elder & Co., 1871.

Brown, Zac, and Wyette Durette, writers. Produced by Zac Brown and Keith Stegall. Performed by Zac Brown Band. "Chicken Fried" (song). Live Nation/Home Grown/Atlantic, 2003.

Byrne, Rhonda. *The Power.* New York: Atria Books, 2010.

———. *The Secret.* New York: Atria Books, 2006.

Chopra, Deepak. *Creating Affluence: The A–Z Steps to a Richer Life.* San Rafael, CA: Amber-Allen Publishing and New World Library, 1993.

———. *The Seven Spiritual Laws of Success: A Practical Guide to the Fulfillment of Your Dreams.* San Rafael, CA: Amber-Allen Publishing and New World Library, 1994.

Coelho, Paulo. *The Alchemist.* New York: Harper Collins, 1998.

Dooley, Mike. *Manifesting Change: It Couldn't Be Easier.* New York: Atria Books, 2010.

Dyer, Wayne W. *Manifest Your Destiny: The Nine Spiritual Principles for Getting Everything You Want.* New York: First HarperPerennial, 1998.

Ford, Debbie. *Courage: Overcoming Fear and Igniting Self-Confidence.* New York: Harper Collins, 2012.

Goldsmith, Barton. *100 Ways to Boost Your Self-Confidence: Believe in Yourself and Others Will Too.* Franklin Lakes, NJ: Career Press, 2010.

Harper, Elizabeth. *Wishing: How to Fulfill Your Heart's Desires.* New York: Atria Books, 2008.

Klingler, Sharon A. *Intuition and Beyond: A Step-by-Step Approach to Discovering Your Inner Voice.* London: Random House UK, 2003.

Krishnamurti, Jiddu. *On Freedom.* Bramdean, UK: Krishnamurti Foundation Trust Ltd., 1991.

Mark, Barbara, and Trudy Griswold. *Angelspeake: How to Talk with Your Angels.* New York: Simon and Schuster, 1995.

Merriam-Webster Dictionary online, http://www.merriam-webster.com/dictionary/request.

Myss, Caroline. *Anatomy of the Spirit: The Seven Stages of Power and Healing.* New York: Three Rivers Press, 1996.

Nelson, Tammy. *What's Eating You?* Oakland, CA: Instant Help Books/New Harbinger Publications, 2008.

———. *Archetypes: Who Are You?* Carlsbad, CA: Hay House, 2013.

Orloff, Judith. *Positive Energy: 10 Extraordinary Prescriptions for Transforming Fatigue, Stress, and Fear into Vibrance, Strength, and Love.* New York: Crown Publishing, 2004.

Peale, Norman Vincent. *The Power of Positive Thinking.* New York: Prentice Hall, 1952.

Peirce, Penney. *The Intuitive Way: The Definitive Guide to Increasing Your Awareness.* Hillsboro, OR: Beyond Words Publishing, 1997.

Robbins, Anthony. *Awaken the Giant Within: How to Take Immediate Control of Your Mental, Emotional, Physical and Financial Destiny!* New York: Free Press, 1991.

———. *Unlimited Power: The New Science of Personal Achievement.* New York: Freepress, 1986.

Tolle, Eckhart. *A New Earth: Awakening to Your Life's Purpose.* New York: Plume, 2005.

Weschcke, Carl Llewellyn, and Joe H. Slate, PhD. *The Llewellyn Complete Book of Psychic Empowerment: A Compendium of Tools & Techniques for Growth & Transformation.* Woodbury, MN: Llewellyn Worldwide, 2011.

Williamson, Marianne. *A Return to Love: Reflections on the Principles of a Course in Miracles.* New York: Harper Collins, 1992.

To Write to the Author

If you wish to contact the author or would like more information about this book, please write to the author in care of Llewellyn Worldwide Ltd. and we will forward your request. Both the author and the publisher appreciate hearing from you and learning of your enjoyment of this book and how it has helped you. Llewellyn Worldwide Ltd. cannot guarantee that every letter written to the author can be answered, but all will be forwarded. Please write to:

Melanie Barnum
℅ Llewellyn Worldwide
2143 Wooddale Drive
Woodbury, MN 55125-2989
Please enclose a self-addressed stamped envelope for reply,
or $1.00 to cover costs. If outside the USA, enclose
an international postal reply coupon.

Many of Llewellyn's authors have websites with additional information and resources. For more information, please visit our website at http://www.llewellyn.com.

GET MORE AT LLEWELLYN.COM

Visit us online to browse hundreds of our books and decks, plus sign up to receive our e-newsletters and exclusive online offers.

- Free tarot readings • Spell-a-Day • Moon phases
- Recipes, spells, and tips • Blogs • Encyclopedia
- Author interviews, articles, and upcoming events

GET SOCIAL WITH LLEWELLYN

 Find us on Facebook

 Follow us on twitter™

www.Facebook.com/LlewellynBooks   www.Twitter.com/Llewellynbooks

GET BOOKS AT LLEWELLYN

LLEWELLYN ORDERING INFORMATION

Order online: Visit our website at www.llewellyn.com to select your books and place an order on our secure server.

Order by phone:
- Call toll free within the U.S. at 1-877-NEW-WRLD (1-877-639-9753)
- Call toll free within Canada at 1-866-NEW-WRLD (1-866-639-9753)
- We accept VISA, MasterCard, and American Express

Order by mail:
Send the full price of your order (MN residents, add 6.875% sales tax) in U.S. funds, plus postage and handling, to: Llewellyn Worldwide, 2143 Wooddale Drive, Woodbury, MN 55125-2989.

POSTAGE AND HANDLING:

STANDARD: (U.S. & Canada)
(Please allow 12 business days)
$25.00 and under, add $4.00.
$25.01 and over, FREE SHIPPING.

INTERNATIONAL ORDERS (airmail only):
$16.00 for one book, plus $3.00 for each additional book.

Visit us online for more shipping options. Prices subject to change.

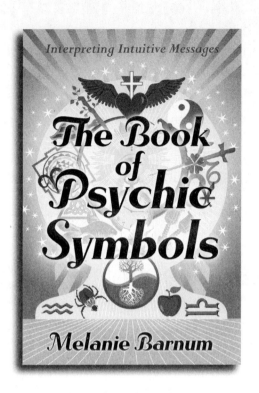

Interpreting Intuitive Messages

The Book of Psychic Symbols

Melanie Barnum

The Book of Psychic Symbols
Interpreting Intuitive Messages
Melanie Barnum

A strong feeling, a remarkable coincidence, a strange dream … What may seem ordinary could actually be an important message—a helpful hint or a warning from a deceased loved one or spirit guide. Open yourself to a wealth of guidance and opportunities by learning how to recognize and interpret the signs and synchronicities all around us.

The Book of Psychic Symbols can help you decode dreams, intuitive flashes, and all psychic impressions. Intuitive counselor Melanie Barnum explains what psychic symbols are, how we receive them, and where they come from. She also shares amazing stories from her life that clarify how the wondrous intuitive process works. In addition to a comprehensive dictionary of 500 symbols, there are many practical exercises for exploring symbols in your life, fortifying your natural intuition, and using psychic symbols to manifest your desires.

978-0-7387-2303-7, 288 pp., 6 x 9   **$15.95**

Melissa Alvarez

365 WAYS

*

to RAISE *Your*

*

FREQUENCY

SIMPLE TOOLS TO INCREASE
YOUR SPIRITUAL ENERGY
FOR BALANCE, PURPOSE, AND JOY

365 Ways to Raise Your Frequency

Simple Tools to Increase Your Spiritual Energy
for Balance, Purpose, and Joy

Melissa Alvarez

The soul's vibrational rate, our spiritual frequency, has a huge impact on our lives. As it increases, so does our capacity to calm the mind, connect with angels and spirit guides, find joy and enlightenment, and achieve what we want in life.

This simple and inspiring guide makes it easy to elevate your spiritual frequency every day. Choose from a variety of ordinary activities, such as singing and cooking. Practice visualization exercises and techniques for reducing negativity, manifesting abundance, tapping into Universal Energy, and connecting with your higher self. Discover how generous actions and a positive attitude can make a difference. You'll also find long-term projects and guidance for boosting your spiritual energy to new heights over a lifetime.

978-0-7387-2740-0, 432 pp., 5 x 7   **$16.95**

To order, call 1-877-NEW-WRLD
Prices subject to change without notice
Order at Llewellyn.com 24 hours a day, 7 days a week!

THE HEALER'S MANUAL

*A Beginner's Guide to Energy Healing
for Yourself and Others*

TED ANDREWS

The Healer's Manual

A Beginner's Guide to Energy Healing for Yourself and Others

TED ANDREWS

Noted healer and author Ted Andrews reveals how unbalanced or blocked emotions, attitudes, and thoughts deplete our natural physical energies and make us more susceptible to illness. *The Healer's Manual* explains specific techniques—involving color, sound, fragrance, herbs, and gemstones—that restore the natural flow of energy. Use the simple practices in this book to activate healing, alleviate aches and pains, and become the healthy person you're meant to be.

978-0-87542-007-3, 264 pp., 6 x 9   **$14.95**

Includes **JOURNEY OF A LIFETIME** *A Self-Directed*
Program of Developmental Actions to "Put it all together"

THE
LLEWELLYN
COMPLETE BOOK
OF
PSYCHIC
EMPOWERMENT

A Compendium of
Tools & Techniques for
Growth & Transformation

CARL LLEWELLYN WESCHCKE
JOE H. SLATE, PH.D.

The Llewellyn Complete Book
of Psychic Empowerment

A Compendium of Tools & Techniques
for Growth & Transformation

CARL LLEWELLYN WESCHCKE

JOE H. SLATE, PHD

Embark on the journey of a lifetime—master the psychic tools and techniques required to develop your highest potential and enjoy success beyond your wildest dreams.

Written by Carl Llewellyn Weschcke and Joe H. Slate, PhD, this book is the most comprehensive guide to psychic development available anywhere. It's a do-it-yourself journey that organizes the concepts of psychic empowerment into a cohesive plan that progresses from positive self-affirmations to powerful step-by-step psychic development techniques. Whether a simple affirmation or an empowering exercise, each technique strengthens the divine spark of greatness existing in everyone—and leads to better health, happier relationships, greater financial success, and enhanced spiritual growth.

978-0-7387-2709-7, 744 pp., 7 x 10   **$29.95**

Garden of Bliss

Cultivating the Inner Landscape
for Self-Discovery

DEBRA MOFFITT

Garden of Bliss

Cultivating the Inner Landscape for Self-Discovery

DEBRA MOFFITT

Garden of Bliss begins on the French Riviera, where Debra Moffitt, despite her glamorous European lifestyle, is unhappy. Realizing that financial success doesn't necessarily equate to happiness, she looks inside herself and decides to make some changes.

The message of her journey is simple: bliss is a destination that exists within all of us. Using the metaphor of a secret garden, Moffitt encourages her readers to manifest this space in the physical world and connect with the divine feminine through nature. *Garden of Bliss* can be read as a stand-alone book or as a companion text to Moffitt's award-winning debut, *Awake in the World.*

"Like *Eat, Pray, Love* without the whine!"—Janna McMahan, bestselling author of *Anonymity* and *The Ocean Inside*

978-0-7387-3382-1, 288 pp., 5³⁄₁₆ x 8   **$16.99**

Foreword by James Van Praagh

YOU
ARE THE
ANSWER

Discovering and Fulfilling
Your Soul's Purpose

Michael J Tamura

You Are the Answer

Discovering and Fulfilling Your Soul's Purpose

Michael J Tamura

World-renowned spiritual teacher, healer, and clairvoyant Michael J Tamura shares his wisdom in this inspirational guide to true spiritual empowerment.

Hailed as a "beautiful manual for living" by Echo Bodine, *You Are the Answer* brings us profound spiritual lessons, highlighted by the author's powerful true stories. Discover how to use your intuition, make room for spirit in your life, and respond—instead of react—to everyday experiences. As you build a temple of the soul, you'll learn to recognize truth, create miracles in your own life, and find your purpose for living!

This insightful and moving guide also features a "spiritual toolkit" of daily practices and exercises to help you on your extraordinary journey in consciousness exploration, healing, and spiritual development.

978-0-7387-1196-6, 288 pp., 6 x 9   **$16.95**

RICHARD
HARVEY

*The Inner Journey to Authenticity
& Spiritual Enlightenment*

Your Essential

SELF

*This book will add needed light to your journey, and help you see
what only the willing heart can see.*
—GUY FINLEY, international bestselling author of *The Secret of Letting Go*

Your Essential Self

The Inner Journey to Authenticity & Spiritual Enlightenment
RICHARD HARVEY

Despite the relationships, possessions, and prestige we all strive for, most people live at only a fraction of their full potential. But with the guidance and wisdom in *Your Essential Self*, you will awaken to your divine nature. Learn how to attain the three stages of human awakening—the process of self-discovery, the transformation into authenticity, and the source of consciousness—on the inner journey to your true self.

This comprehensive guide describes how spiritual attainment is not an unreachable fantasy, but rather a logical extension of human development. The personality, the authentic self, and the transcendent self are discovered through stories from Richard Harvey's personal experience, case studies from his therapy practice, questionnaires, and exercises designed for your journey toward self-realization.

978-0-7387-3470-5, 288 pp., 6 x 9 **$15.99**